Practical Partnership

Practical Partnership

Caroline Harmer

of the Middle Temple, Barrister
Principal Lecturer at The College of Law, Guildford

Peter Camp LL B

Solicitor, John Mackrell Prizeman
Senior Lecturer at The College of Law, Guildford

© Oyez Longman Publishing Limited 1982
Norwich House, 11/13 Norwich Street
London EC4A 1AB

ISBN 0 85120 663 8

All rights reserved. No part of this publication may be reproduced, stored in a retrieval system, or transmitted, in any form or by any means, electronic, mechanical, photocopying, recording or otherwise, without the prior permission of the publishers.

Set in Times and Univers
and printed in Great Britain by
The Eastern Press Limited of London and Reading

Contents

Preface

For some time now there has been a need for a book on professional partnerships. The standard books on partnership deal with partnership law admirably, but do not deal with the more practical aspects of setting up and running a firm. What we have attempted to do in this book is, in Part I, to look briefly at the law as it applies to partnerships generally, and then in Part II to apply the law to professional partnerships, with special reference to solicitors' partnerships. We are thus not concerned with the subject of limited partnerships. The chapter on taxation in Part I amounts to a bird's eye view of the subject: it should not be treated as an exhaustive coverage of the topic, but more as an introduction to or a reminder on revenue law. Taxation then appears in context in Parts II and III of the book. In Part II in addition to applying the law to solicitors' partnerships, we look at many practical aspects of setting up and running a firm. We consider financial matters such as the provision of initial finance, accounts and how to provide a retiring partner with his capital and any share of the assets. Day to day matters considered include office efficiency and management of the firm. Wherever relevant such topics as taxation and Solicitors' Practice Rules appear in context. Part III of the book deals with choice of business medium. It is included because, although it does not strictly relate to the setting up of a solicitor's firm, it is an important part of the advice that a solicitor provides for his business client. We have incorporated changes proposed in the current Finance Bill, anticipating the enactment of the Finance Act 1982, but otherwise the law is stated as at 1 March 1982.

We are indebted to Mr Peter Purton for his permission (and the permission of his publishers, Messrs Oyez Longman) to reproduce the partnership deed in Appendix 3 which is taken from the loose-leaf work *Organisation and Management of a Solicitor's Practice.*

It has been slightly shortened to make it more appropriate for a small or medium size firm. We are also indebted to our colleagues at The College of Law for their encouragement and help. In particular we would thank Richard Holbrook without whose belief that 'you will never do it', the book would not have been completed. We would also like to record our thanks to our patient and helpful publishers.

We have throughout the book for convenience referred to a partner as 'he', although we hope that this will not discourage those of the opposite sex who are or aspire to be partners.

March 1982

PJC
CGH

Table of Cases

Table of Statutes

Table of Rules

Statutory Instruments

Law Society Rules

Part I

General Principles

Chapter 1

Definition and Nature of Partnership

1 Introduction

What is a partnership? Very generally, it is where two or more people work together in a business or profession. They are not employer and employee, one is not sub-contracted to the other; they work on more or less equal terms to make a success of their joint endeavour.

Partnership is defined by the Partnership Act 1890, which is the main Act concerned with partnership law. It codified much of the then existing law which has, since that time, suffered little amendment either by statute or court decisions. However, s 46 provides that 'the rules of equity and common law applicable to partnership shall continue in force except so far as they are inconsistent with the express provisions of this Act'. Consequently, many pre-1890 cases are still useful to interpret the provisions of the Act or are still good law despite the Act. Unlike much modern legislation the 1890 Act, which is set out in Appendix 1, is short and easily understandable. Having said that, however, it must be remembered that the rules governing the partnership relationship exist partly as a result of the Act and in many cases partly as a result of the agreement entered into by the partners themselves which may amplify or override the provisions of the Act. The written agreement is known as partnership articles.

One of the matters that the parties cannot override by agreement is the legal definition of partnership. They either are partners according to the law, or they are not. They cannot agree to become partners in the future if they are already within the definition, and they cannot expressly declare that they are not partners and hope to avoid the obligations of partnership if they are partners (*Pawsey* v *Armstrong* (1881) 18 Ch D 698). If there is a partnership, certain obligations are imposed on partners in their dealings with each other; and, perhaps more important, each partner becomes able to bind the firm in contracts with third parties, each partner becomes fully liable to those third parties for the debts of the firm, and the partnership may be liable for a partner's tortious act committed in the course of the firm's business. Where the partners are plaintiffs rather than defendants, they may sue in the firm's name.

2 Definition of partnership

Section 1 of the 1890 Act defines partnership as 'the relation which subsists between persons carrying on a business in common with a view of profit'. From that it can be seen that there must first of all be a business. This is defined as including 'every trade, occupation or profession' by s 45. However, this definition is not conclusive. There are certain limitations, eg a barrister is not allowed by the rules of his profession to enter into partnership with another barrister. The word 'occupation' causes some difficulty. It has to be construed *eiusdem generis* with the other words, and therefore although persons may be occupied in doing something, they will not be partners unless the undertaking has some commercial characteristics. As Brett J put it in *Smith* v *Anderson* (1880) 15 Ch D 247 there has to be 'a series of acts which if successful will produce gain'. To give an example, two brothers who are landowners together and who occupy themselves in looking after the land, managing it and preserving it, are not necessarily partners unless they run a business on the land, when they may be partners in the profits from the land alone, or if the land is essential to the business, partners as to the land as well (see s 2(1); *Davis* v *Davis* [1894] 1 Ch 393; *Waterer* v *Waterer* (1873) LR 15 Eq 402).

3 Evidence of partnership

The business does not have to be a long-term one. People who work together for one single purpose or deal can still be partners: they are known as a syndicate or consortium. The business does, however, have to be in existence for the partnership to exist. The words in s 1 are 'carrying on a business'; thus if people plan to set up a partnership in the future to run a restaurant, they are not partners until the restaurant is actually in being. While they are preparing for its opening, by ordering goods and opening the bank account for example, they are not partners (see *Keith Spicer Ltd* v *Mansell* [1970] 1 WLR 333).

There are no formalities which have to be completed to bring a partnership into being. No forms have to be filled in, no notifications need be given, no documents need be drawn up. This is very different from starting a company, a point which is considered in more detail in Part III of this book. In many cases, however, the partners will want to get an agreement drawn up and in some circumstances registration may be necessary (for VAT purposes for example).

Very often the question of whether persons are partners or not arises because one person is unable to pay off his business debts; his creditor then looks elsewhere to see if there is anyone else who might be liable. If the creditor can find another person who is a partner, then that person will be liable for the business debts (this is more fully discussed in Chapter 2). Alternatively an individual who is faced with having to pay a large amount of money to the creditor may attempt to bring in a person he believes is his business associate and therefore should be partly responsible for the firm's debts. Section 2 of the Act was drafted with these problems in mind. Section 2(1) states that 'Joint tenancy, tenancy in common, joint property, common property, or part ownership does not of itself create a partnership as to anything so held or owned, whether the tenants or owners do or do not share any profits made by the use thereof'. Because of s 2(1) co-owners can agree to be partners in the profits made from the property but remain co-owners only as to the property itself. Further, if they buy additional property with the profits, it will be held as co-owners and not as partners (see s 20(3)). If therefore two or more people own land in common, a partnership may not be in existence. Looking at it from another point of view, if people run a business, the place where they carry on the business, although co-owned, may not necessarily be partnership property. All of this is important in deciding whether partnership rights and obligations exist in the first place, and then whether the property is part of the business and should be sold, or inherited as such (see p 52).

Although many of the problems are likely to involve land, there is a nice case about a racehorse. In *French* v *Styring* (1857) 5 WR 561 a racehorse was purchased by several persons whose aim was to share in the ultimate winnings of the horse, ie they were to be partners as to the profits from this horse. As is so often the case in racing, their hopes were not fulfilled and it became a question of how the debts were to be shared and paid. In this respect it was important to decide if they were partners as to the horse and thus whether it was partnership property. It was decided they were not (and s 2(1) later reflected this approach). The judge, showing as many do a very good understanding of the horse, pointed out that it would have been different if the horse was to be used for breeding purposes, because there the ownership and the business were inseparable.

Section 2(2) provides that the sharing of gross returns does not of itself create a partnership As we shall see, the essence of partnership is sharing net returns. If two friends decide to purchase and sell a consignment of goods, split the proceeds and each pay their own expenses, they are not partners but two sole traders. In *Lyon* v *Knowles* (1864) 5 B & S 751 one person owned a theatre, the other a theatrical company. The theatrical company presented plays at this theatre and the arrangement was that they split the box-office takings. A creditor, bearing in mind that the theatre owner would be more likely to be able to pay off debts if necessary by selling or mortgaging the theatre itself, would want both persons declared partners so that the theatre owner would be liable for debts incurred by the theatre company. However, in a case such as *Lyon* v *Knowles* they would not be partners simply by virtue of sharing gross returns; something else would have to be found to show they were carrying on a business in common.

Section 2(3) provides that 'the receipt by a person of a share of the profits of a business is prima facie evidence that he is a partner in the business. . . .' The subsection makes it clear that sharing net profits is not conclusive evidence of partnership. Subject, however, to the exceptions noted below, sharing net profits will give rise to a presumption of partnership which will place the burden of proof on the person who is attempting to deny the existence of partnership.

(*a*) *Five statutory exceptions to general rule that sharing net profits creates a partnership*

(*1*) *Paying off a debt by instalments out of the profits (s 2(3)(a)).* This exception stems from the case of *Cox* v *Hickman* (1860) 8 HL Cas 268. That case arose because a trader ran into debt. His creditors were faced with two possibilities: first, putting him out of business but only getting paid a proportion of what they were owed because there would not be enough to enable them to be paid completely; and second, letting him retain the business but taking a share of the profits each year until the debts were paid off. Obviously the trader had to be left with a share of the profits too, otherwise he would have been unable to put any money back into the business or even have any money to live on. The creditors chose the second alternative and trustees were appointed to supervise the business and distribute the profits. The creditors were now sharing net profits. Were they also partners? If so they would also share any losses and be fully liable for any other of the firm's debts. The answer was no. The situation in the case is still of relevance today even though the ways of enforcing judgment have changed somewhat since 1860. Two modern ways of enforcing judgment are to appoint a receiver by way of equitable execution, who will do very much what the trustee did in *Cox* v *Hickman*, and to enter into a scheme of administration.

(2) *Paying a servant or agent out of the profits (s 2(3)(b))*. It has for a long time been an accepted way of paying an employee to make him part of some profit-sharing scheme. If all such employees became partners as soon as they took a share of net profits, the situation would be intolerable and the Act merely recognises this. In a solicitors' practice it is common for the employees to be given a bonus out of the profits, eg at Christmas (but see r 3 of the Solicitors' Practice Rules 1936–72, p 71).

(3) *An annuity, paid out of the profits, for the widow or child of a deceased partner (s 2(3)(c))*. In many cases, the partners will make provision for such an annuity in the partnership agreement. If there is no agreement, they may consider agreeing to an annuity after the death of the partner. This annuity is an illustration of the relationship that should exist between partners whereby they are prepared to support not only each other but dependants as well. By being in receipt of a proportion of net profits the widow (or widower: Interpretation Act 1978, s 6) and children do not become partners, nor are they likely to want to be. Section 2(3)(*c*) however protects them from the creditor who seeks to sue them for the firm's debts.

(4) *The payment of interest on a loan out of net profits (s 2(3)(d))*. Section 2(3)(*d*) is of particular importance to those involved in trading rather than professional partnerships:

> The advance of money by way of a loan to a person engaged or about to engage in any business on a contract with that person that the lender shall receive a rate of interest varying with the profits, or shall receive a share of the profits arising from carrying on the business, does not of itself make the lender a partner with the person or persons carrying on the business or

liable as such. Provided that the contract is in writing, and signed by or on behalf of all the parties thereto.

Let us use as an example a person who wishes to start a small business. He needs £10,000 to set it up, to buy the necessary equipment. He also needs a certain amount of working capital, to pay himself until the business is on its feet, to pay his staff if any, and to pay rent. The bank is prepared to finance the latter but not the former. He goes to a friend who is prepared to invest £10,000 in this new business but does not want to help in running the business and wants to make sure that his liability will not exceed the £10,000 if the business fails disastrously. The friend is prepared to wait to be paid any interest until the business is making profits and happy to wait until the end of each year to see what the trader can afford to pay him. It is essential therefore that they do not inadvertently become partners. The friend wants to be in the position of a shareholder in a company, although he will have fewer rights.

Section 2(3)(*d*) allows interest to be paid out of the profits without creating a partnership. This includes taking a share, eg 10% pa of the profits where the share does not vary but the actual amount does, or taking a varying amount each year depending on agreement between them. If, by the way, the friend is to be paid only a fixed rate of interest, eg 10% pa on the loan, then he is a creditor like any other. In order to make sure that s 2(3)(*d*) applies a contract between lender and borrower must be drawn up, it must be in writing and signed by or on behalf of all the parties. This must be a loan contract. Anyone drawing up such a contract should be careful that it does not have the appearance of partnership articles, otherwise it may do the very thing it was designed to avoid—namely create a partnership. Thus, it is advisable to avoid a clause where the interest to be paid is in the same ratio as the loan money is to the firm's capital—if the lender has put in £2,000 and the borrower has put in £18,000, the lender should not be paid 10% of the profits. Arbitration clauses are not often found in loan contracts, but are common in partnership agreements and so should not be included, nor should any clause which gives the lender a right to take part in the running of the business. If there is an argument as to whether the lender has become a partner, then it would appear that if there is not a loan contract, he will be presumed to be one; if there is a contract the court will look at all the details of it to see whether a partnership has been created. Thus, in *Pooley* v *Driver* (1876) 5 Ch 458 where the lender was expressed to have a share in the capital of the firm, a right to a share in the profits and a right to insist that the partners did a good job, it was held that a partnership existed.

A word of warning to those who lend money, even though a perfect loan contract is drawn up: if the lender actually takes part in the running of the business, perhaps because he is worried his money is not being properly used or protected, then the court will, if it feels that a business is being carried on in common, hold that a partnership exists (*Stewart* v *Buchanan* (1903) 6 F (Court of Session Cases) 15).

The lender should be warned of the effect of s 3 of the Act which provides that if the firm becomes insolvent, the claims of the lender are postponed to those of the ordinary unsecured creditor. Thus he ranks last in the list to be paid off. After him come only the proprietors themselves. He has to wait until, eg the milkman has been paid. He should therefore find out if it is possible for him to be given any security, eg a second charge on the trader's house. If that is the case then his claim (for both interest and the capital sum provided the contract is properly drawn) ranks above the unsecured creditor's. A point which will be discussed in more detail when considering business medium but can be mentioned here is that it is more difficult for a sole trader or partnership to give security because they cannot, as a company can, create a floating charge; they will have to have some fixed asset which can be charged, eg a private house, or business premises.

The lender should therefore be advised of three things:

1 Ensure that a proper loan contract is drawn up and correctly signed.
2 Take no part in the running of the business however tempting it may be to try to protect his money. He is entitled to be told the state of the firm's business however and the contract can carefully define his rights.
3 Take some security if at all possible.

(5) *Payment for goodwill out of the profits (s 2(3)(e)).* When a business is sold it is common for a valuation to be put on the premises and equipment, and then a separate value to be put on the goodwill, ie the reputation of the firm, the profit-making capacity of the firm. One of the ways of paying for the goodwill is out of the very profits it is supposed to create, over a period of time (eg by way of an annuity), or perhaps in a few lump sums over the first year. The outgoing businessman does not thereby become a partner with the incoming one (see *Pratt* v *Strick* (1932) 17 TC 459 where a

doctor sold goodwill in this way, but note that today doctors are not allowed to sell goodwill by virtue of the National Health Service Act 1947). In these circumstances s 3 will again apply and the seller ranks after the unsecured creditors.

(b) Professional considerations

In most professional relationships, where the financial considerations are very different to those in trading contexts, disputes about whether a partnership exists are rare. However, the question may arise as to exactly when a partner becomes a partner (*Waddington* v *O'Callaghan* (1931) 16 TC 187) or whether a partner is a salaried partner or a full partner (see *Stekel* v *Ellice* [1973] 1 WLR 191, which is discussed at p 132).

Chapter 2

Liability of Partners to Third Parties

1 Contract

Whilst in law the partnership is not a distinct legal entity, when dealing with the partners' contractual liability it is helpful to consider the firm as the principal and each partner as an agent of the firm.

Section 5 of the Partnership Act 1890 states that:

> Every partner is an agent of the firm and his other partners for the purpose of the business of the partnership; and the acts of every partner who does any act for carrying on in the usual way of business of the kind carried on by the firm of which he is a member bind the firm and his partners, unless the partner so acting has in fact no authority to act for the firm in the particular matter, and the person with whom he is dealing either knows that he has no authority, or does not know or believe him to be a partner.

The effect of s 5 is that each partner has authority to bind the firm unless this authority has been restricted by agreement with his co-partners. It is therefore a form of both actual and usual authority. Problems occur when the partner's authority has been restricted and despite this he enters into a contract on behalf of the partnership with a third party. If this is the case the third party will have no constructive notice of the restriction since there is no requirement for the partners to register their articles of partnership. Therefore unless the third party has actual notice of the restriction, he will be able to sue the partnership on the contract, providing the act of the transgressing partner falls within the scope of the usual way of business of the firm. Where, however, the third party has notice of the restriction, s 8 provides that an act done by a partner in contravention of the restriction will not be binding on the firm.

In *Mercantile Credit Co Ltd* v *Garrod* [1962] 3 All ER 1103 a partnership was formed for the purpose of carrying on a garage business concerned with letting lock-up garages and repairing cars. *P* was concerned with the management of the business, *G* was merely a sleeping partner. The partnership deed excluded the partners' rights to buy and sell cars. *P*, without *G*'s authority, sold a car to which he had no title to the plaintiff finance company. The company paid *P* £700. When the company discovered that *P* had no title, it claimed the £700 from *G*. The company succeeded in its claim since the act of *P* fell within s 5 and the partnership was consequently liable.

The question which must be asked in each case is whether the act of the partner falls within the scope of the usual way of business of the firm. This will obviously vary in each case according to the type of business the firm does. However, the courts have laid down certain principles over the years and it is now possible broadly to categorise certain matters that will and will not fall within such scope.

In all partnerships it is within the scope of a partner's usual authority to buy and sell goods in relation to the firm's business, to engage or dismiss employees, and to give receipts in respect of payment of debts owed to the firm. In addition to these matters, if the partnership is a trading concern (ie where the principal operation is the buying and selling of goods) the scope of a partner's usual authority is extended. In the case of *Bank of Australasia* v *Breillat* (1847) 6 Moo PCC 152 the Privy Council listed matters which are in the scope of such a partner's authority. A trading partner may borrow money on behalf of the firm, deal in any way in negotiable instruments in the name of the firm, pledge any goods belonging to the firm and create an equitable mortgage by deposit of the title deeds to property owned by the firm.

There is also case law dealing with matters which are never within the scope of the usual way of business of the firm. Thus, a partner has no authority to execute a deed on behalf of the firm (eg a legal mortgage) (*Berkeley* v *Hardy* (1826) 5 B & C 355); to give a guarantee in the firm's name (unless it is customary in that trade) (*Brettel* v *Williams* (1849) 4 Exch 623); he may not accept property in lieu of money owed to the firm (*Niemann* v *Niemann* (1890) 43 Ch D 198); and he cannot submit any dispute between the partners to arbitration (*Stead* v *Salt* (1825) 3 Bing 101). It must be remembered that although a partner does not have usual authority for these acts, it is possible for his co-partners expressly to authorise him to carry out these acts on behalf of the partnership.

Finally, in relation to s 5 it should be noted that despite the fact that a partner who has no authority is acting in the usual way of business, a third party who does not know or believe him to be a partner will have no contractual rights against the firm.

2 Tort

The basic principle is that the partnership is liable for wrongs committed by one partner against a third party in the ordinary course of the firm's business.

Section 10 of the Partnership Act 1890 states that:

> Where, by any wrongful act or omission of any partner acting in the ordinary course of business of the firm, or with the authority of his co-partners, loss or injury is caused to any person not being a partner in the firm, or any penalty is incurred, the firm is liable therefor to the same extent as the partner so acting or omitting to act.

For the firm (and thus all the partners) to be liable under s 10 the wrong must be committed either with the authority of the co-partners or where the partner is acting in the ordinary course of the business of the firm. Thus a solicitor who is a partner and who is guilty of negligence in the course of the firm's business will not only be personally liable to the client but will also render his fellow partners liable. In *Hamlyn* v *Houston & Co* [1903] 1 KB 81 a partner in the firm bribed a clerk in a rival firm into giving him confidential information. It was held by the Court of Appeal that the partnership was liable for the wrong committed by the partner in inducing a breach of contract since it was within the ordinary course of business for a firm to seek commercial information concerning a rival. It was immaterial that such information had been sought in such a way as to constitute a tort.

Section 11 of the Partnership Act 1890 deals with the specific case of misappropriation of a third party's money or property and states:

> In the following cases namely—
> (*a*) where one partner acting within the scope of his apparent authority receives the money or property of a third person and misapplies it; and
> (*b*) where a firm in the course of its business receives money or property of a third person and the money or property so received is misapplied by one or more of the partners while it is in the custody of the firm;
>
> the firm is liable to make good the loss.

The section deals with two situations. The important distinction between them is that whereas in (*a*) the partner must be acting within the scope of his apparent authority, in (*b*) the firm must merely receive the money in the course of its business. The Act does not use the words 'the ordinary course of business'. Therefore if money is misappropriated from the firm's custody, the firm need not have received the money in the ordinary course of its business for all partners to be liable. Practically, the distinction between (*a*) and (*b*) has little effect, since it is within a partner's usual authority to give receipts for debts owed to and money received by the firm. Consequently, if one partner receives the money, and misapplies it this will generally fall within (*b*).

There are a number of cases on the effect of a partner's apparent authority but most of these predate the Partnership Act. It is useful, however, to know what the courts have viewed as within a partner's apparent authority. For example, in the case of *Blair* v *Bromley* (1847) 16 LJ Ch 495 money was paid to a firm of solicitors for investment in a specific security. One partner misappropriated the money and it was held that in receiving the money the solicitor was acting within his apparent authority and consequently the firm (and therefore the innocent partner) was liable to the client. Whilst old cases can be useful, care must be taken when relying on them as authorities since the very nature of, for example, a solicitor's partnership has changed since the last century. What was not within a partner's apparent authority then may well be within it today.

Examples of what the courts have considered to be beyond the partner's authority (and therefore following misappropriation the firm and partners have not been liable) include concealed receipt by a solicitor of bearer bonds deposited for safe custody (*Cleather* v *Twisden* (1884) 27 Ch D 340); the receipt of mortgage moneys from the borrower without the consent of the lender, who was a client of the firm (*Sims* v *Brutton* (1850) 5 Exch 802); and the unauthorised removal of securities from a bank where they were deposited for safe-keeping (*Ex p Eyre* (1842) 1 Ph 227).

3 Joint or joint and several liability

The Partnership Act 1890 provides that in the case of contractual debts and obligations incurred by the firm every partner is jointly liable with his other partners (s 9) and in the case of liability incurred by the firm for the tort of a partner under ss 10 and 11 the liability of the partners shall be joint and several (s 12). The importance of the distinction was that where the liability was joint, once a third person had obtained judgment against any of the partners he was then barred from commencing any further claim on the same cause of action. However, the distinction has no importance in connection with contracts made after 1 January 1979. The reason for this is s 3 of the Civil Liability (Contribution) Act 1978 which provides as follows:

> Judgment recovered against any person liable in respect of any debt or damage shall not be a bar to an action, or to the continuance of an action, against any other person who is (apart from any such bar) jointly liable with him in respect of the same debt or damage.

It follows that if a third party brings an action to judgment against, eg two partners in a three partner firm, and that judgment is not satisfied, he can now bring a further action on the same contract against the third partner provided s 3 of the 1978 Act applies.

If the cause of action arose from one partner's tort in circumstances where the firm was liable, since the liability is joint and several, the same problems did not apply. Consequently the 1978 Act has not affected the third party's rights where those rights are in tort.

4 Suing the firm

Because the partnership is not a separate legal entity as is a company, it has no separate personality to sue. Thus prima facie all the partners must be joined in the same action if the plaintiff is to have the possibility of enforcing the judgment against all of them, or they will have to be sued one by one. In either case the increased cost and inconvenience are great. The Rules of the Supreme Court, Ord 81, and the County Court Rules, Ord 5, allow the firm to be sued in the firm name.

Before suing in the firm name, however, the plaintiff is advised to find out who the partners are and whether they are worth suing. Further research may be necessary to discover the financial position of the firm and the individual partners. In addition, the Rules (RSC, Ord 81, r 2) provide that those joined in the firm name can be compelled to disclose the names and addresses of all the members who make up the firm.

The action is started by writ in the High Court and summons in the county court. In each case the firm name is used to indicate the defendant. The writ or summons is effected by serving it on any one or more of the partners, or by leaving it at their principal place of business with the person having control or management of the business or appearing to have control at the time of service (r 3 ibid). Thus it is not necessary to gather all the partners together to effect due service (except after the firm has been dissolved to the knowledge of the plaintiff (r 3(2)). The person so served with a writ must be given written notice of the capacity in which he is served, eg whether as partner or person with control. If no notice is given he will be deemed to be served as a partner.

The firm must then acknowledge service in the High Court and give notice of intention to defend within fourteen days. If a solicitor has not been instructed the acknowledgement of service form must be completed by a partner by name, with the words in Paragraph I of the form 'partner in the firm of X'. Thereafter the action proceeds in both courts in the normal way.

Once judgment has been given against a firm, then special rules apply to the enforcement of the judgment. If the partners are sued in their own names then judgment cannot be enforced against the firm's property as such, but only against their share of the firm's property. Judgment against the firm in the firm name allows execution of it by writ of fi fa or by warrant against the firm's property (s 23(1) of the Partnership Act). Partnership property cannot be seized in execution of a judgment unless that judgment is against the firm. Rule 5 of RSC, Ord 81 provides that execution to enforce judgment can issue against any of the firm's property within the jurisdiction and against the private property of any person acknowledged as a partner, or served as a partner. In addition, execution may issue against the private property of any other person against whom judgment is entered and who is liable to satisfy that judgment as a partner in the firm. This can only be done with leave of the court and it has to be proved that he was a partner at the time the judgment debt was incurred. Thus by suing in the firm name, the plaintiff who obtains judgment is able to enforce it not only against the firm's property but also against the private property of all the partners, although leave of the court may be necessary in some cases.

A particular method of enforcing judgments against partners is the charging order. Charging orders are now governed by the Charging Orders Act 1979. The charging order operates in two stages: the judgment creditor applies to the court for a charging order; on application an order is made which can then be confirmed or made absolute at the subsequent hearing. The effect of the order is that there is a charge in favour of the judgment creditor over the partner's share of the partnership assets. If the charging order does not have the effect of producing the money to satisfy the judgment debt, then the creditor can go back to the court and ask for the sale of the defaulting partner's share of the assets. If the court makes the order then the partnership assets will have to be sold. The remaining partners have various options. They can pay the debt and then seek to recover the money from the defaulting partner—in this way they can at least ensure the continuance of the firm. Or, under s 33(2) of the Partnership Act, they can dissolve the partnership, as the charging order does not dissolve the firm automatically.

5 Insolvency

If the firm does not have sufficient assets to pay its debts then it is insolvent. If the firm is insolvent then so also are all the partners in that firm. Thus there will be joint creditors for the partnership debts and separate creditors for the debts of each individual partner. The Bankruptcy Act 1914 contains rules for keeping these two sets of creditors apart. Section 33(6) of the Act provides that the joint estate (ie the partnership assets) must be applied first in paying off the joint creditors and the estates of the individual partners must first be applied in paying off that individual's private creditors. If the joint creditors have been fully paid, then the private creditors can look to the remaining partnership assets for payment; similarly it is not until the private creditors have been fully paid that the firm's creditors can pursue their remedy against the private estates of the individual partners. There are certain exceptions to these rules, eg if there is no joint estate at all then the joint creditors may proceed against the separate estates of the individual partners on the same footing as the private creditors. It is, however, extremely unlikely that there will be no joint estate—even the existence of a table, chair and typewriter constitutes one.

If one partner goes bankrupt then this dissolves the firm unless the articles state otherwise (see p 50). The joint creditors will be paid off by the solvent partners and then both the solvent partners and the individual's creditors will wish to prove against the separate partner's estate. The general rule is that a partner cannot prove against either the joint estate or the bankrupt partner's estate in competition with the firm's creditors. As long as the firm's creditors have been paid in full the solvent partners can prove against the bankrupt partner's estate.

If the bankruptcy does not dissolve the partnership, the individual's trustee in bankruptcy is the assignee of the bankrupt partner's share in the partnership assets. He does not have the right to take part in the management of the firm but he is entitled to the bankrupt partner's share of the profits; on a dissolution he is entitled to that partner's share (s 31 of the Partnership Act). In practice, it is likely that the solvent partners will wish to purchase the bankrupt partner's share and so relieve the partnership from the problems created by the bankruptcy. There are also special rules which apply if the solvent partners wish to prove in the bankruptcy for debts due to them in respect of the partnership (see above).

6 Duration of liability

The basic rule is that a partner is only liable for debts and obligations of his firm which were incurred whilst he was a partner. Section 17 makes this clear:

> (1) A person who is admitted as a partner into an existing firm does not thereby become liable to the creditors of the firm for anything done before he became a partner.
>
> (2) A partner who retires from a firm does not thereby cease to be liable for partnership debts or obligations incurred before his retirement.

In *Court* v *Berlin* [1897] 2 QB 396 a solicitor was engaged by a partnership to institute proceedings on behalf of the partnership for the recovery of a debt. Before the proceedings were concluded two of the partners in the partnership retired. When the solicitor sued all the partners for his costs the court held that the retired partners were liable for the costs including those incurred after their retirement. The solicitor's retainer was an 'entire contract' and thus he did not have to obtain fresh instructions at each step in the proceedings.

This basic rule, however, can be overruled in circumstances where all three parties contract to this effect. Such a contract is called novation, and is a tripartite contract between, for example, the creditor of the firm, the retiring partner and the existing partners, relieving the retiring partner from his liability for the debt owed to the creditor. Like any other contract, to be enforceable there must be consideration. It is important to remember that although in many cases where one partner retires the continuing partners may expressly indemnify him against existing and future debts of the firm, this indemnity will not affect a creditor's rights unless he is a party to a contract of novation. Section 17(3) gives statutory recognition to a contract of novation in relation to retiring partners, and states that such a contract 'may be either express or inferred as a fact from the course of dealing between creditors and the firm as newly constituted'.

Partners about to retire from the firm must have particular regard to two further sections of the Act.

Section 14(1) provides that:

> Every one who by words spoken or written or by conduct represents himself, or who knowingly suffers himself to be represented, as a partner in a particular firm, is liable as a partner to anyone who has on the faith of such representation given credit to the firm, whether the representation has or has not been made or communicated to the person so giving credit by or with the knowledge of the apparent partner making the representation or suffering it to be made.

The subsection is self-explanatory and as can be seen it would apply equally to a retiring partner or someone who has never been a partner. The usual way it applies in practice is where a partner who has retired fails to remove his name from the headed notepaper of the firm. If a third party gives credit to the firm on the faith of the representation on the headed notepaper, then that ex-partner is liable as an apparent partner, if he knows of its use. Under s 14(1) it is quite clear that an apparent partner will only be liable if he 'represents himself or knowingly suffers himself to be represented as a partner. . . .' Therefore a retiring partner is not liable under s 14 where he arranges with his partners that, for example, the stock of notepaper will be destroyed, but nevertheless in breach of that arrangement the paper is subsequently used. The last part of s 14(1) clearly covers the situation where *A* represents to *B* that he is a partner in a particular firm, and *B* communicates that fact (without *A*'s knowledge) to *C*, who gives credit to the firm on the faith of that representation. Clearly *A* would be liable to *C* under s 14(1) in these circumstances.

The second section of the Partnership Act which has particular relevance to retiring partners is s 36. This provides:

> (1) Where a person deals with a firm after a change in its constitution he is entitled to treat all apparent members of the old firm as still being members of the firm until he has notice of the change.
>
> (2) An advertisement in the London Gazette as to a firm whose principal place of business is in England or Wales. . . . shall be notice as

to persons who had no dealings with the firm before the date of the dissolution or change so advertised.

(3) The estate of a partner who dies, or who becomes bankrupt or of a partner who, not having been known to the person dealing with the firm to be a partner, retires from the firm is not liable for partnership debts contracted after the date of the death, bankruptcy or retirement respectively.

A retiring partner should therefore be familiar with the consequences of three different types of person dealing with the firm after his retirement. Persons dealing with the firm, who also dealt with it before his retirement, should be circulated with actual notice of his retirement. It is, however, assumed that proper headed notepaper satisfying the provisions of ss 28–31 of the Companies Act 1981 would amount to actual notice (see p 72). Persons who had not dealt with the firm before his retirement but nevertheless knew him to be a partner should be given constructive notice. The retiring partner should give notice of his retirement in the *London Gazette.* No notice is required for those persons who had not dealt with the firm, and had not known him to be a partner. Following his retirement, the partner will not be liable for partnership debts incurred with such persons after his retirement. See *Tower Cabinet Co Ltd* v *Ingram* [1949] 2 KB 397 which also deals with the question of 'holding out' under s 14.

In relation to both s 14(1) and s 36 the effect of *Scarf* v *Jardine* (1882) 7 App Cas 345 is important. Suppose that *A* and *B* are in partnership. *A* retires and on the same day *C* joins *B* as a partner. *A* fails to give proper notice within s 36 and a third person (*T*) contracts with the firm after the change in the firm's constitution. *T* in that situation must elect between enforcing the contract against either *A* and *B* (on the basis that they were apparent partners within s 36) or against *B* and *C* (the actual partners when the debt was incurred). *T* has no rights against all three jointly.

Sections 36(3) and 14(2) deal with the position of a partner's estate following his death. Section 36(3) states that his estate is not liable for debts incurred after the partner's death and therefore there is no requirement for notice of the death to be given to, for example, existing customers of the firm. Section 14(2) states that:

Provided that where after a partner's death the partnership business is continued in the old firm-name, the continued use of that name, or of the deceased partner's name as part thereof shall not of itself make his executors or administrators estate or effects liable for any partnership debts contracted after his death.

So where the firm name is Jones & Co, the death of Jones and the continued use of his name will not make Jones's estate liable.

Finally, it has been seen that a partner's authority to act on behalf of the firm stems from s 5 and his position as a partner. Following dissolution of the partnership, an individual's authority will continue for a limited time despite the fact that he is no longer a partner. Section 38 provides:

> After the dissolution of a partnership the authority of each partner to bind the firm, and the other rights and obligations of the partners, continue notwithstanding the dissolution so far as may be necessary to wind up the affairs of the partnership, and to complete transactions begun but unfinished at the time of the dissolution, but not otherwise.
>
> Provided that the firm is in no case bound by the acts of a partner who has become bankrupt; but this proviso does not affect the liability of any person who has after the bankruptcy represented himself or knowingly suffered himself to be represented as a partner of the bankrupt.

Chapter 3

The Duty of Good Faith

1 Introduction

A fundamental characteristic of a partnership is the duty of good faith that exists between the partners. It is a duty to behave towards each other with the utmost fairness. It is a duty which overrides all other considerations. In practice it is the reason why many people may decide to run a business as a partnership rather than as a company, believing that the duty of good faith (and the fact that each partner is liable to his last shilling and his last acre for the partnership debts) will mean that each person will put his or her best efforts into the business. Unfortunately in some cases it is the reason why at the outset of the business partnership articles are not thought necessary. The lack of a partnership agreement can cause serious problems later on if there is a disagreement, or when a partner is leaving the firm.

The duty of good faith as it applies to partnerships is a development of a basic principle of equity. The partners are in a fiduciary position as regards each other. As Roskill LJ said in *IDC Ltd* v *Cooley* [1972] 1 WLR 443, 'It is an overriding principle of equity that a man must not be allowed to put himself in a position in which his fiduciary duty and his interests conflict.' Although, as we shall see, ss 28–30 of the Partnership Act reinforce the duty, it is not wholly dependent on statute and exists irrespective of any agreement between the parties.

2 Consequences of breach

In *Law* v *Law* [1905] 1 Ch 140 William and James were partners in a wool business in Halifax. William lived in London and took little part in the running of the business. When James offered to buy his share in the partnership at what seemed to be a fair price bearing in mind all that William knew about the business, he accepted. However, James, because of his more detailed acquaintance with the business, had certain facts within his exclusive knowledge—namely the existence of certain partnership assets. William had therefore sold his share at an undervalue. When he discovered this he sued James and the court held that the contract between them was voidable for non-disclosure. This was an application of the *uberrimae fidei* principle, or as it is called in relation to partnership, the duty of good faith.

A more recent application of the duty of good faith can be seen in *Floydd* v *Cheney* [1970] Ch 602. The firm concerned was a firm of architects. While one partner was abroad on holiday, with his thoughts anywhere but on the business, the other was busy copying documents and indeed, it appeared, removing originals. When the first partner returned to the office after his holiday he was informed that the other was leaving. The court ordered the return of the documents and issued an injunction to stop use being made of the confidential information in them. To use the firm's documents for one's own purposes was a clear breach of the duty of good faith. There was, in this case, some dispute about whether the defendant was actually a partner or merely waiting to become one, but the duty of good faith would seem to extend to persons negotiating for a partnership.

The duty of good faith could also be said to stretch out beyond the grave. An example of this is the case of *Thompson's Trustee* v *Heaton* [1974] 1 WLR 605. *T* and *H* were partners and acquired the lease of a farm. The partnership was dissolved in 1952. However, with *T*'s consent, *H* continued to live at the farm although the occupation was later passed to *H & Co Ltd*, a company controlled by Mr and Mrs *H*. The leasehold interest had never been changed and was therefore an undistributed asset of the former partnership. In 1966 Mr *H* died and a year later his executors bought the reversion which they sold four years later at a considerable profit. *T* sought a declaration that the executors held the reversion on trust for *H Ltd* and *T*. By the time the case came to court *T* had died. The court held that the reversion and any profit was still partnership property, even though the partnership had been dissolved so many years before, and ordered it to be divided between the two estates.

3 Partnership Act provisions

Section 28 of the 1890 Act provides that:

> Partners are bound to render true accounts and full information on all things affecting the partnership to any partner or his legal representative.

If for any reason information is withheld from one partner then any agreement between them can be set aside, not only an agreement to sell as in *Law* v *Law* (above) but also an agreement as to the internal running of the partnership.

Section 29(1) provides that:

> Every partner must account to the firm for any benefit derived by him without the consent of the other partners from any transaction concerning the partnership, or from any use by him of the partnership property, name or business connection.

A partner must not make a secret profit whether made innocently or not. If he does so he can be ordered to render a true account of it and it will be brought into the partnership profits and thus shared out between all the partners. An old case illustrates the point. In *Bentley* v *Craven* (1853) 18 Beav 75 the defendant was a buyer for a firm of sugar refiners. Instead of going straight to the sugar sellers on behalf of the firm, he bought a consignment of sugar at a low price in his personal capacity, waited until the price rose and then sold it to the firm without disclosing his true identity. He was ordered to account to the firm for the profit he had made.

What happens if in the course of business a partner hears that a good contract is up for tender or that a consignment of goods is for sale at a low price and that partner in his personal capacity takes the contract (see *IDC Ltd* v *Cooley* [1972] 1 WLR 443, a company case based on the same principle) or buys the goods (*Bentley* v *Craven*)? It matters not that the firm might not have wanted the contract or the goods, or that they could not have got the contract or the goods without the defendant. The fact that he has used his business or professional knowledge, skill and contacts means that he has to account to the firm. If a partner should find himself in this position, he should disclose to the other partners that this is the case and get their agreement that he should go ahead on a personal basis. Only in this way is the duty of good faith satisfied.

Leases can lead to problems. If a lease is a partnership asset (whether in the firm's name or an individual partner's name, see p 76) then a single partner who renews it or purchases its reversion does not hold it for himself only but as trustee for the partnership.

In addition, if he should sell the reversion, any profit he makes must be brought into the firm's account (see *Thompson's Trustee* v *Heaton; Protheroe* v *Protheroe* [1968] 1 WLR 519).

Section 29(2) extends the rules to profits made after a dissolution due to the death of a partner but before final settlement of the accounts. Thus any profit made by the remaining partner or partners or by the representatives of the deceased partner between dissolution and final settlement not only is a partnership profit but must also be taken into account in settling the deceased partner's share of the partnership (*Clements* v *Hall* (1858) 24 Beav 333).

Section 30 deals with the problems of a partner setting up or taking part in a competing business.

> If a partner, without the consent of the other partners, carries on any business of the same nature as and competing with that of the firm, he must account for and pay over to the firm all profits made by him in that business.

Section 30 is only infringed if the business is carried on without consent and is actually competing with the existing partnership. Thus unless it is competing both in nature and in fact, that is for the same clientele, the partner's business is outside the scope of the section. If a firm in London is in business selling spare parts for cars and one partner opens a spare car parts business in Carlisle, the two businesses, although similar in nature, are not actually in competition because they are not selling to the same customers (unless of course the trade is exceptionally specialised). Similarly, if the partner opens a greengrocery business two doors down the road, the two businesses are not competing because they are of a different nature. The partner who is part of the other business does not have to account for profits of it to the existing firm under s 30. He might, however, have to account for profits under s 29 because it will be very likely that he has used some of the firm's connections. In *Aas* v *Benham* [1891] 2 Ch 244 a partner who was a shipbroker started a shipbuilding company. It was held that he was not carrying on a competing business and therefore need not account for profits made. Further, since he was not making a profit out of the firm's name, no relief was granted under s 29. However, the court did grant an injunction restraining him from making use of the firm's name for his own purposes in the future.

Of course, if he is spending a lot of time on the new business, even if it is not competing, a partner cannot be devoting all his time to the partnership and may be in breach of the partnership articles.

There may be a case for considering the expulsion of that partner or for dissolving the partnership, by going to the court if necessary (see p 51). There may be a case for suing the partner for damages and/or an injunction for breach of the partnership articles. In addition, if in setting up his new business he has used the firm's name, property or connections then s 29(1) applies and in that way he may be asked to account for some or all of the profits. (When talking about competing businesses, it is worth pointing out that competition can be just as damaging to the existing firm when a partner leaves and then sets up a competing business. The partnership articles therefore often contain a clause restraining such competition because s 30 does not cover this situation.)

If one partner is thought to be causing such problems that it would be better if he left, one of the ways of bringing about his leaving is to expel him from the partnership. If the partnership articles so provide (see s 25 and p 95), then the expulsion can be put into effect by majority decision. The decision must have been motivated by a desire to further the interests of the business or profession and not the partners themselves. The duty of good faith applies to this decision as it does to all others. In *Blisset* v *Daniel* (1853) 10 Hare 493 a partner was expelled in accordance with the articles but for the wrong reasons. He had annoyed one of the other partners by objecting to that partner's son being appointed to the firm. He had been induced to sign accounts, which were then binding on him, so that his share could be bought at a low value. The court found that he was being expelled because of personal animosity and not for the good of the firm and ordered that his expulsion be set aside.

Looking at the type of business carried on by a solicitor, it seems that he might have to consider the duty of good faith, eg where he is asked to become a director of a company for which he has done work as a solicitor; where he runs a company; where he buys property from or through a client or where he invests in a business run by a client.

Chapter 4

Taxation: General Principles

1 Introduction

All businesses, whether they be trading businesses or professional ones and whether they be formed as companies or partnerships or consist of the sole trader or practitioner, are subject to income and capital taxes, but in differing ways. A knowledge of the relevant tax rules is very important to those running or advising a business.

Tax cannot be raised except by authority of an Act of Parliament or, more exceptionally, by subordinate legislation. Taxes on income are annual taxes and thus an annual Finance Act is necessary to make the collecting of taxes legal. Capital taxes do not need annual authorisation. Rates of tax can be changed immediately by virtue of statute, once a budget resolution has been passed by the House of Commons. As might be imagined, case law abounds on the precise interpretation of the very detailed and complex tax legislation. Statutes must be precisely interpreted because no tax can be imposed except through clear statutory words. Any ambiguities must be resolved in favour of the taxpayer. At present the main statutes are the Income and Corporation Taxes Act 1970 and subsequent Finance Acts; the Capital Gains Tax Act 1979 and the Finance Act 1975 (which introduced Capital Transfer Tax (CTT)). A company is taxed on its income profits but the tax it pays is known as corporation tax; a sole trader or a partnership is taxed on income profits and pays income tax; all three may, in buying and selling assets, make capital gains which are subject to tax; a company cannot be liable to CTT but the sole trader who gives away his business, or the partner who gives away his share of the business, may be liable to CTT.

2 Income tax

Section 1 of the Income and Corporation Taxes Act 1970 charges tax for each year of assessment on all property, profits or gains, described or comprised in the schedules to the Act. The schedules lay down what comprises income within each of them and how exactly profits are to be calculated, ie what is to be treated as a receipt of income and what can be deducted from it as expenditure. If a profit does not fall within the schedules then it is not income to be taxed; it may nevertheless be a capital profit and subject to a capital tax. Schedule A charges tax on annual profits or gains arising in respect of certain rents or receipts from land in the United Kingdom. (The United Kingdom is defined as England, Wales, Scotland and Northern Ireland; it does not include the Channel Islands and the Isle of Man which have their own and more favourable tax laws.) Schedule B charges tax on certain income from woodlands. Schedule C charges certain profits from public revenue dividends.

Schedule D brings into the charge to tax the profits of a trade (Case I); the profits of a profession or vocation (Case II); interest, annuities, annual payments (Case III); certain other income (Cases IV–VI). This is the schedule with which we shall be particularly concerned.

Schedule E charges income arising from offices, employment and pensions. An employee will be taxed under this schedule as will the director of a company and so in most cases will an ex-partner receiving a pension.

Schedule F charges dividends and other distributions made by companies resident in the United Kingdom.

Certain income is specifically made exempt from tax, eg scholarship income, child benefit and income of a charity.

(*a*) *The calculation of tax*

The first thing that has to be done is to work out how much income is subject to tax. Let us take as an example an individual who is running his own small business which is not a company. He is also a non-executive director of his brother's company and he has several shareholdings on which he receives dividends. We have already involved Schedules D, E and F. We could give him a house or flats which he lets and an expanse of woodlands in deepest Wales and bring in A and B but perhaps that would be too ambitious.

The income arising under each schedule must first be calculated.

This is done by applying the particular rules of each schedule to find the income that is brought into the charge to tax. Thus the statutory income of the business under Schedule D will be the receipts of the business less allowable expenditure, any loss relief and capital allowances (it is not the amount drawn from the business by the individual); that of Schedule E will be the gross earnings (and any perks) less allowable expenditure which has a much more limited meaning in this schedule; the dividends and tax credits received will form the statutory income for Schedule F. The income of these three schedules is added together and amounts to the aggregate statutory income for this particular individual.

The statutory income of an individual is not the amount on which he is taxed; the reason for this is that certain payments made by him are allowed to be set off against it. These payments are called charges on income. They are deducted from the aggregate statutory income to arrive at a person's total income. This is not the place for a discussion of some of the complicated provisions relating to charges on income, but to illustrate what is meant here are some of the payments which are charges on income. First, interest but not capital payments on a mortgage taken out to buy or improve a person's only or main residence qualify for relief. This relief is available for interest paid on loans up to £25,000. A similar relief is available for interest paid on a loan to enable an individual to buy a share in a partnership or to pay capital or a premium or an advance to and for the use of the partnership. Here, however, there is no maximum. The main rules on interest relief are to be found in the Finance Act 1972, s 75. Other charges on income include small maintenance payments and other maintenance payments paid net of basic rate tax under an agreement or court order. These charges on income can be set off against the top of the individual's earnings so that if he has income which is being taxed at 60% (or even 75% if investment income surcharge is being paid) they will first reduce this income. Another type of charge on income is what is known as an annual payment, eg a covenant to a charity. To be an annual payment the payment must have the quality of pure profit income in the recipient's hands, ie it must not be paid for services or goods rendered; it must have the quality of recurrence and it must be capable of lasting for more than six years. (Except that where charities are concerned the minimum period has been reduced to three years: Finance Act 1980, s 55(1).) If this is so then it has a special tax treatment which is beneficial to the payer. The covenant to a charity falls within the definition of an annual payment as does an annuity to great-aunt Maud. The annual payment is a charge on income. If the agreement is to pay £100 a year to the charity then this can be set against the payer's income for tax purposes; unlike the charges on income so far discussed, however, it can only be set against that part of his income that is subject to basic rate tax; it cannot be used to avoid higher rate tax. So the £100 is removed from the payer's income; for the purposes of easy collection of tax, however, the payer is directed by the Act to pay to the recipient an amount net of basic rate tax, ie £70 in our example (while the basic rate of tax is 30%). He is then supposed to hand over the £30 tax to the Revenue. However, because his income is going to be taxed anyway, it will not be necessary to go through this rather elaborate procedure. He will agree to pay to the charity such sum as after deduction of tax at the basic rate will amount to £70 and then certify that this has been paid out of taxed income. This achieves the same result as described above. The charity on receiving the £70 net of basic rate tax and not being a taxpayer will then make a repayment claim and get back the £30 tax paid on its behalf by the covenantor. Thus the covenantor by paying the charity £70 has managed to give it £100. This is of advantage to the payer because otherwise he would have had to pay £100 out of income that had already been taxed. Certain annual payments are, by s 457 of the Income and Corporation Taxes Act 1970, made charges on income for higher rate tax purposes as well. These are annuities to retired partners and their families made under a partnership agreement (see p 156), annual payments made in connection with the purchase of the whole or part of a business (subject to certain conditions) and payments on divorce, nullity or separation. From 6 April 1981, covenants to charity which do not exceed £3,000 in any year of assessment are also included in this list.

Further examples of charges on income are qualifying premiums on buying a retirement annuity (ie a pension) and paying for a pension through a pension scheme. Such premiums can be set against 'relevant earnings' which generally means the earnings of that employment to which the pension relates. They cannot be set, eg, against investment income (see p 91).

All this is done to arrive at an individual's 'total income'. Against his total income his personal reliefs can be set to arrive at his taxable income. The main personal reliefs are as follows: the single person's allowance (for 1982/83 this is £1,565)—all single persons including children can set this against any earned or unearned income; the married man's allowance—if a husband and wife are living together in the year of assessment then this higher allowance (£2,445) can be claimed; in addition if the wife is working there is the wife's earned income allowance that can be claimed which is equivalent to a single person's allowance. There are other allowances, eg additional personal allowances.

Once the taxable income has been calculated, then and only then can the amount of tax payable be worked out. Income is taxed on a gradually increasing scale. The first £12,800 is taxed at 30% (the basic rate). Thereafter it increases gradually until the top rate of 60% is reached at £30,501. If, however, any of the income is unearned income, eg dividend income, then once it exceeds £6,250 it has applied to it what is known as the investment income surcharge, ie a further 15% tax. The highest rate of tax in this country can be 75% on a proportion of a person's income. If any of the income has been taxed at source (eg the dividend income which was included gross (ie dividend and tax credit) in our example although it was received net of the equivalent of basic rate tax) then credit must be given for that. The net figure of tax is finally arrived at.

How is this calculation done? At the end of each year of assessment a return has to be made to the inspector of taxes. This is done by completing a form that the individual will be sent on which he gives all the relevant information. The year of assessment for an individual runs from 6 April in one year to 5 April in the next. The dates are curious and one of the reasons suggested for their use is that when the calendar was changed, the people thought that they had lost eleven days on which they were being taxed. The present tax year may have been fixed to appease them.

(b) The computation of profit under Schedule D

The profits of a trade, profession or vocation are computed according to the rules in Schedule D. Schedule D, Case I covers the profits of a trade, and Case II those of a profession or vocation. This is so whether the business is carried on by a sole trader, a partnership or a company (although there are certain differences where the latter is concerned).

Much case law is devoted to whether a person or persons are carrying on a trade, profession or vocation (usually the former). The reason for this is that if it can be shown that the income did not so derive then it cannot be an income profit, and is, if anything, a capital profit where the top rate of tax is 30% and not 60%. Where an individual purchased one million rolls of lavatory paper in

Berlin, and brought them to England and then sold them, he was held to be trading even though he was concerned with only one consignment of goods. It could not be said that the purchase was for the purpose of investment or for his own personal use (*Rutledge* v *IRC* (1929) 14 TC 490). However, in this context we are concerned with established businesses whether of a trading or professional nature and *Rutledge*-type arguments are unlikely to apply.

Tax is charged on the annual profits or gains of the trade, profession or vocation. The Revenue will accept the business accounts for the purpose of assessing tax subject to certain adjustments that have to be made, eg for capital allowances. The basic formula for calculating the profit is that taxable receipts less allowable expenditure will amount to profit for tax purposes; this can then be adjusted to take account of any stock relief, loss relief and capital allowances that are available.

The taxable receipts in any year will be the sums earned in that year. This is known as the 'earnings basis' of accounting. It means that a trader or more importantly a professional man will have brought into the charge to tax (1) the work that has been done and paid for, (2) the work that has been billed and not yet paid for, and (3) work done but not yet billed. (As we shall see, the Revenue will in some cases allow what is known as a cash or bills delivered basis: pp 116–118.) In addition to sums earned during the year, there are rules and cases whereby certain other sums may be treated as trading receipts, eg compensation for cancellation of a business contract (*Kelsall Parsons & Co* v *IRC* (1938) 21 TC 608); non-returnable deposits on uncollected goods (*Elson* v *Prices Tailors Ltd* (1962) 40 TC 671); market value of goods disposed of to a trader (*Sharkey* v *Wernher* [1956] AC 58). Any sum which is received as capital rather than income is not brought into account for the purpose of calculating income profits; it is, however, relevant for the purpose of calculating capital profits and capital taxes, eg where freehold premises in which the business is carried on are sold.

Where the earnings basis of accounting is used this involves calculating the value of work in progress or, eg, the partly manufactured goods and unsold stock. In a trading partnership the value of stock or raw materials has to be calculated at the beginning and end of the accounting period. It is valued at cost or market price whichever is the lower. The reason for doing this is that in the trading account the partnership is trying to establish the true profit element of the receipts during the year (the gross profit). The profit is obviously the sums earned during the year less the costs of the goods sold during the year. Where stock is constantly going in and out of a business it can be imagined that it would be impossible to calculate each item individually. Thus opening and closing stock are valued to arrive at the cost of goods sold, and thereby the gross profit.

Example:

Trading Account
Year ending 31 December 198–

	£	£	£
Sales			120,000
Less cost of sales			
Opening stock	20,000		
Add purchases	80,000	100,000	
Less closing stock		30,000	70,000
GROSS PROFIT			50,000

Because of this calculation, if the value of stock increases during the year, due not to an increase in the amount of stock but to inflation, a higher gross profit is made, ie the higher the closing stock the higher the profit. The trader is thus paying tax on inflation.

The government in 1975 introduced a system of stock relief to help the trader. The relief merely deferred tax, but companies and individuals were building up such a deferred tax liability due to the ever present rates of inflation that subsequent Finance Acts provided for some of the deferred tax to be written off. The Finance Act 1981 introduced an entirely new system of stock relief based on a published government index. In most cases this now is a true relief and not a deferment of tax liability. In addition all deferred tax has been written off.

Having arrived at a figure for gross profit, then in the profit and loss account expenses are deducted to discover the net profit figure. Deductible trading expenditure is limited for tax purposes to expenditure, that is revenue rather than capital expenditure, and to that which is incurred wholly and exclusively for the purposes of the trade. Expenditure made once and for all is likely to be capital expenditure, eg money paid out to add an extension to the freehold premises. Recurrent expenditure is likely to be income expenditure, eg rates and rent. Capital expenditure is regarded as being made with a view to bringing into existence an asset or an advantage for the enduring benefit of the trade, whereas revenue (or income) expenditure enables the businessman to run his business from day to day. By s 130 of the Income and Corporation Taxes Act 1970, expenditure that is not wholly and exclusively for the purposes of the trade, etc, is disallowed, as is expenditure on maintaining the partners, their families or their establishments. Where expenditure is laid out for a dual purpose it is not wholly deductible, although the Revenue will allow a proportion. For example, rent of premises used partly for business and partly for domestic purposes will be split so that the rent of the part used solely for business purposes becomes a deductible expense. The most usual items of deductible expenditure are rent, rates, repairs to buildings, equipment, salaries, compensation and redundancy payments, pension contributions, entertaining overseas customers, legal and professional charges (but not for the purchase of capital items), travelling on business (but not travelling from home to work), and interest.

Once a net profit has been established there are further reliefs.

Capital allowances. Although capital expenditure is not a deductible business expense for the purpose of calculating income profits, there are various allowances which can be set against income profits on the purchase or improvement of certain capital assets. The aim of these allowances is to encourage industry and business to modernise and expand. Thus there are allowances available in respect of expenditure on machinery and plant, industrial building and agricultural building (*inter alia*). The nature of the allowance differs according to what is purchased. As an example, if a trader buys a piece of machinery (eg a typewriter) he can set anything up to the whole cost of it off against profits in the first year; any balance remaining can be allowed in the second and subsequent years as a writing down allowance of 25% of the unclaimed cost of the piece of machinery. If he should sell the machinery, what he gets for it has to be brought into the charge to tax if, as is likely, he has already claimed an allowance for it. There is a special system of allowances for cars other than for commercial use: there is no first year allowance, but limited writing down allowances may be claimed.

Stock relief. As previously indicated, a certain sum will be set against taxable profits.

Loss relief. If the business has made a loss in earlier years this can be carried forward to the present year and be set against profits of the same trade or profession (Income and Corporation Taxes Act 1970, s 171). Any unrelieved loss can be carried forward in this way indefinitely. As an alternative, the loss can be relieved under s 168 of the Income and Corporation Taxes Act. This allows the loss to be set against any income of the taxpayer in the year of the loss (s 168(1)), or against any income in the following year (s 168(2)). The advantage of using s 168 instead of s 171 is that it allows *any* income of the trader to be relieved, not just the income from the loss making business. However, s 168 can only be used if it is shown that there was an expectation of the business making a profit. The taxpayer can elect to have his loss relieved under s 168, and any unrelieved loss can then be relieved under s 171. Any loss made in the last twelve months of the trade or profession can be carried back and set against certain earlier profits (Income and Corporation Taxes Act 1970, s 174). There are also rules which allow losses made in the early years of a business to be carried back to income made before the business began (Finance Act 1978, s 30).

(*c*) *The preceding year basis*

All that has been said so far relates to the computation of profit during the year in question. But what is the year in question? Inevitably it is not possible to calculate a firm's profits until some time after the given period has come to an end because of the difficulties in finding out the necessary information and the time it takes to draw up accounts. In addition the firm's accounting period may be eg 1 January to 31 December while the year of assessment for tax purposes is 6 April to 5 April. The preceding year basis of assessment is that the profits to be taxed in the current tax year will be the profits of the firm's financial year which ended in the preceding tax year. Thus if the firm has made up its accounts for the calendar year 1981, this will form the basis of assessment for the year of assessment 1982/83.

When a new business opens, it is self evident that the preceding year basis cannot be used; there are therefore special rules that apply to the opening year of a business. In the year of assessment when a business begins, tax is charged on the actual profits during that year of assessment. In the next year of assessment tax is charged on the profits of the first twelve months of trading, and in the third year of assessment the normal preceding year basis of assessment is used.

Example:

A business opens 1 October 1981:

For year of assessment 1981/82 profits of 1 October 1981 to 5 April 1982 are used;

for year of assessment 1982/83 profits of 1 October 1981 to 30 September 1982 are used;
for year of assessment 1983/84 profits of 1 October 1981 to 30 September 1982 are used.

It can be seen that the profits of all or part of the first year of the firm form the profits for tax purposes in the first three years of assessment. That is why it is often said that it is sensible to make a loss in the first twelve months: no tax will be paid for at least three years. As there is always a lot of capital expenditure at the beginning of a business and there may be large capital allowances to be claimed, a loss can very often be shown. By the Finance Act 1978, s 30, any loss in the first four years of assessment can be set against the profits of an earlier business, or the loss can be carried forward and set against future profits, or it can be carried across as earlier described.

The taxpayer has the right to elect that the second and third years be taxed on the actual profits made in those years of assessment, and he has seven years after the second year of assessment in which to make the election.

At the end of the business, the actual profits of the final year of assessment are charged to tax during that year. So if the business ends on 31 May, nearly two months' profits will be charged to tax. For the two earlier years (the penultimate and ante-penultimate) an assessment will have already been made on a preceding year basis. This will stand unless the Revenue elect to tax actual profits during those years, which they will do if this calculation produces higher profit figures.

The opening and closing year rules are important to remember when looking at changes in the constitution of a partnership (see p 141).

(*d*) *Comparison of Schedule D with Schedule E*

A person who is in employment, ie employed under a contract of service, or a person who holds an office, eg a director, is taxed on the emoluments of that employment or office. He is taxed on those sums that derive from his employment (see *Jarrold* v *Boustead* [1964] 1 WLR 1357), which are defined to include salaries, fees, wages and other perquisites. The latter include pensions, and other reward in money or money's worth. A lower paid employee is taxed only on those perks that can be converted into money, eg second-hand value of a suit, but not free meals. A higher paid employee or director (ie whose emoluments including perks exceed

£8,500 pa) is taxed on all perks whether or not they can be converted into money, and he is taxed on them on what it costs his employer to provide them. In addition there are special rules which apply to cars for higher paid employees and directors. They are taxed according to an amount laid down by statute which depends on the engine capacity of the car and its age and cost. These rules are very detailed and are outlined here only for the sake of comparison.

Under Schedule E travelling expenses can be set off against earnings for tax purposes if they were incurred necessarily for the purposes of the employment; other expenses are only deductible if they were incurred wholly, exclusively and necessarily in the performance of the employee's duties. This is a narrower test than that in Schedule D.

Schedule E emoluments have basic and higher rate tax deducted at source, ie by the employer under the PAYE system, according to the recipient's code number, which depends on the particular personal reliefs and interest and other reliefs available to him.

Several important differences between an employee of the firm and the person or persons running the firm should be noted. An employee receives earnings net of tax; a person running the business receives any money taken out of the business and any other profits the firm makes, gross, and tax has to be paid later.

Expenditure that can be set off in the firm's accounts is far wider—it is not essential to prove that it was necessarily incurred.

Those things which are perks under Schedule E and therefore taxed, eg the car, are deductible for tax purposes under Schedule D, so not only does the owner of the business not have to pay tax if the firm buys a car for his use, but also it reduces the net profits on which he pays tax because of capital allowances.

Under the PAYE system an employee pays his tax monthly or weekly, depending on how he is paid, throughout the year; at the end of the year of assessment he should not, unless he has a lot of other income, have any further tax to pay; the owner of the business will have to pay tax later and will have to remember to set some money aside for the tax payments which fall due on 1 January and 1 July (see p 122).

Income is taxed under Schedule E on a current year basis, but on a preceding year basis under Schedule D.

3 Company taxation

A company's profits are computed in very much the same way as an individual's or partnership's profits. The normal schedules apply except in so far as they cannot apply to a company, eg personal reliefs for individuals are ignored. A company that is trading has its profits computed under Schedule D, Case I; a company that is managing land has its profits computed under Schedule A. A company does not pay income tax; it pays corporation tax on both its income and capital profits, whether distributed or not, eg whether distributed as dividends to shareholders or not. The rate of corporation tax is fixed in arrears and applies from 1 April to 31 March. Where a company's accounting year does not coincide with this financial year and there is a change in the rates of tax, the profits must be apportioned on a time basis to discover which rate of tax applies to what proportion of profits. As capital gains are taxed at 30%, a proportion of them only is brought into the charge to corporation tax to ensure that they do not suffer a higher rate than 30%, ie 15/26ths of capital profits are charged to tax.

There is a measure of relief for small companies. A special rate of corporation tax applies to companies whose profits do not exceed £90,000; the rate is 40%. Between £90,000 and £225,000 the overall rate gradually increases from 40% to 52%. This only applies to profits of an income nature.

Corporation tax is payable within nine months of the end of the period for which it is assessed, ie the company's accounting year. However, where the company makes a qualifying distribution, eg pays a dividend, during an accounting period, it is liable to make a payment of advance corporation tax (ACT) to the Revenue which will later be set against its liability to corporation tax. The amount of ACT payable is at present 3/7ths of the distribution. Thus if the company wishes to pay a dividend to its shareholders amounting in total to £7,000, ACT of 3/7 × £7000, ie £3,000, must be paid. It is important to realise that this means if a company wishes to pay £7,000 to its shareholders it must have £10,000 available. When a company makes a distribution of profits or any assets that could have been used for dividends or, eg, sells assets at an undervalue to shareholders, then ACT is payable. If the company makes a repayment of share or loan *capital* this is not a distribution and is not subject to ACT.

Anyone who is making a study of company taxation should

realise that there are special rules relating to the treatment of charges on income, capital allowances and loss relief. They are not, however, within the scope of this book.

A director of a company receives fees which are taxed under Schedule E, being the emoluments of an office. These, provided they are wholly and exclusively incurred for the purposes of the company, ie are not too high, are deductible in assessing profits for corporation tax purposes. If a director receives a dividend it is subjected to basic and possibly higher rate tax under Schedule F (as is a dividend paid to any shareholder) and may be liable to the investment income surcharge if dividends are in excess of £6,250. However, because of the fact that the company has paid the equivalent of basic rate tax on it in the form of ACT, he receives the dividend plus a 'tax credit'. His liability to basic rate tax is then satisfied and any excess liability can be calculated. Payment of dividends is not a deductible expense in computing a company's profits for corporation tax purposes.

Where a small company is concerned, special rules apply. This is because the financial organisation of the company is in the hands of those who stand most to benefit from their own decisions as to distribution of profit; eg directors and shareholders are often the same persons. There are thus certain anti-avoidance provisions which apply to what are known as close companies.

Close companies are companies under the control of five or fewer participators, or of participators of any number who are directors. Control means having majority voting power or a major financial interest, or being entitled to more than half the company's income. A participator is someone who has a share or interest in capital or income of the company, including someone who is entitled to acquire shares or voting rights. Any rights of an associate or nominee of a participator must be attributed to the participator. Associates include close relatives. A private family company is thus likely to be within this definition. If a father and his son and daughter are directors and between them they have 51% of the shares, the company is under the control of five or fewer participators; it is no good them giving shares to their spouses or their children to avoid the definition, because as they are their associates, their interests will be attributed to the directors or participators.

If a company is a close company, then the definition of distribution is extended to include, eg, providing living accommodation or other benefits in kind for a participator or his associate (unless already taxable under Scheme E). Thus if, eg, a director's sister is given a house, this amounts to a distribution with the result that the company must pay ACT and the sister must pay excess tax (higher rate and investment income surcharge) on the distribution.

Loans to participators or their associates (unless made in the ordinary course of the business or to a full time director with no material interest) are treated in a special way. If, eg, a director's son wishes to start a business and is lent £10,000, a sum equivalent to ACT will have to be paid, but as the loan is not a distribution, the sum cannot be set against the company's corporation tax liability. When the loan is repaid the sum is recoverable; if the loan is released or written off, the borrower is charged to excess tax on the grossed up amount of the loan.

If a company withholds income from distribution its members (shareholders) will not pay income tax on that income (although it will already have suffered corporation tax). In a close company the people who decide to withhold income (the directors) are also likely to be the major shareholders. Thus rules existed so that such undistributed income was in certain cases treated as if it had been distributed; it was apportioned between the shareholders who were then taxed on it. The Finance Act 1980, s 44, has abolished these rules in relation to trading income of a trading company. The Revenue still have the power to apportion the non-trading income of a trading company, or the income of a non-trading company.

4 Capital gains tax

CGT is levied on the total amount of chargeable gains which accrue to a person on the disposal of chargeable assets in a year of assessment (or accounting period in the case of a company). In calculating the total amount of chargeable gains allowable losses can be deducted. The Capital Gains Tax Act 1979 contains the main provisions relating to individuals.

(*a*) *The calculation of tax*

The first point to consider is whether there has been a disposal. Unless there has, no capital gains tax problem can possibly arise. Disposal is not defined but it will cover the sale or gift of an asset (or part of it, eg land, when special rules are used to calculate any gain). The 1979 Act extends the ordinary meaning of the word disposal to cover certain other situations thus bringing them within the CGT rules. Section 20(1) extends the meaning of the word to cover, eg, capital sums received by way of compensation for any kind of damage or injury to assets, or for their loss (inter alia). If property is destroyed by fire and insurance moneys are received then this is treated as a disposal and the difference between what the property cost and the money received will amount to the capital gain. If no money is received, because the property was not insured, then an allowable loss has been made. A point for the trader to remember is that if he appropriates a business asset for his own use (or a personal asset for business use) then this is a disposal. So if he takes over the office premises for his own private use, there will have been a disposal to him from the business at market value (deemed) on which he will have to pay CGT unless one of the reliefs apply.

The disposal has to be of a chargeable asset. This includes land, currency other than sterling, and property created by the person disposing of it, eg a building that he has erected. Private motor cars are not chargeable assets nor is any tangible moveable property that is a wasting asset, eg office furniture. Special rules apply to the calculation of a gain on other wasting assets (eg a lease for fifty years or less).

If there has been a disposal of a chargeable asset then the gain or loss must be calculated. The acquisition or base cost of the asset, the cost of any improvements to it and the cost of acquisition and disposal (eg legal costs, etc) are deducted from the consideration received to arrive at the chargeable gain, or loss. The Finance Act 1982 introduces a system of index linking for the calculation of gains so as to avoid in future the taxation of gains resulting from inflation. This does not apply to gains made before March 1982, nor to gains in the first year of ownership. All the CGT examples below are, however, shown, for the sake of clarity, without the index-linking provisions being applied.

Chargeable capital gains are subject to CGT at a rate of 30% (s 3). However, for individuals (and personal representatives in the year of assessment when death occurred and the following two tax years) the first £5,000 of the net gain in any tax year is exempt from CGT (Finance Act 1980, s 77). For trustees of most settlements there is a reduced exemption of £1,500 pa subject to certain conditions (*ibid*, s 78).

If a loss is made on any disposals which if profitable would have been charged to CGT, then the loss goes to reduce any gain in that year. If an overall loss is made in the year of assessment then it can be carried forward without time limit (but not back or across to income profits) and set against gains over £5,000; it is not set against gains of £5,000 or less in any year, so as to protect the £5,000 exemption (Capital Gains Tax Act 1979, s 5). A capital loss on unquoted shares in a trading company can be set against any income tax liability (Finance Act 1980, s 37).

CGT is assessed on a current year basis and is payable on or before 1 December in the following year of assessment (Capital Gains Tax Act 1979, s 7).

Transfers between husband and wife are deemed to produce no gain or loss; thus the acquiring spouse takes over the disposing spouse's assets at the original acquisition cost and CGT is deferred. This applies while husband and wife are living together (see s 44).

CGT is not payable on disposals on death.

(*b*) *Exemptions and reliefs*

Chattels (*s 128*). If chattels are sold or disposed of for £2,000 or less, no CGT is payable on any gain. Special rules apply for calculating the gain where the consideration is more than £2,000.

Private residences (*s 101*). Any gain realised by an individual on the disposal of his only or main residence is exempt from CGT subject to certain conditions.

Life assurance policies (*s 143*). If a person takes out a policy of life assurance, no CGT arises on payment of the policy moneys to the policy holder (or to his personal representatives, as CGT is not payable on death) or to the trustees of a voluntary settlement to whom the assured has transferred the policy. However, if the policy is assigned the exemption does not apply.

Tangible moveable property (*s 127*). Tangible moveable property that is also a wasting asset (ie if the asset has a predictable life of fifty years or less), eg office machinery, the office yacht, is exempt from CGT.

Replacement of business assets (*s 115*). Where a person or firm sells business assets, ie those used solely for trade or professional purposes, he is allowed to defer paying CGT until a later date provided certain conditions are fulfilled. This is not an exemption from CGT, it is merely a relief which allows CGT to be delayed because the capital gain is rolled over into the next assets; hence its popular name 'roll over relief'. If the trader puts the whole of the consideration (ie the sale price) for the old business assets into the acquisition of new business assets, then he can claim the relief. Relief is given by allowing the trader to deduct the gain in calculating the sum paid for the new assets. The result is that the acquisition cost of the new asset is lower than its actual cost and thus when the trader finally sells the asset without replacing it, he will have made a greater gain for the purposes of tax than he actually has made on this particular sale.

Example:
A trader buys freehold premises in 1970 for £25,000 and sells them in 1975 for £35,000, so that he can move to bigger premises. He pays £50,000 for the new premises which he keeps until he sells the business in 1982, when the premises are worth £70,000. He will pay no CGT when he sells in 1975; however, the acquisition cost of the new premises for CGT purposes will, instead of being £50,000, be deemed to be £50,000 less the gain made on selling the first premises of £10,000. Thus the acquisition cost of the new premises is £40,000, and the gain which is chargeable to CGT in 1982 is £30,000. It has been rolled over until the final sale.

For this relief to apply, the old and the new assets must be within the classes of assets laid down by the Act. The classes are: buildings or structures occupied and used solely for the purposes of the trade, land so used and occupied, fixed plant and machinery; ships; aircraft; goodwill; hovercraft (see s 118).

If less than the whole consideration for the old asset is applied in buying the new one, then there is a limited relief provided the amount that is not put towards the new asset does not exceed the gain on the old asset (s 116).

Retirement relief (s 124). Where an individual has reached sixty years then s 124 of the Act provides relief from CGT where there is a disposal by sale or by gift of the whole or part of the business; or of shares or securities of a company. Certain conditions have to be fulfilled throughout at least one year ending with the disposal, if the relief is to apply. These conditions are, inter alia, that the business which is being disposed of either wholly or in part is owned either by an individual, or it is owned by a company and:

(i) it is a trading company;
(ii) it is the individual's family company; and
(iii) the individual is a full time working director.

An individual's family company is defined as a company where either he holds at least 25% of the voting rights, or he and members of his family together hold at least 51% of the voting rights, no less than 5% being exercisable by the individual.

The amount of relief that can be claimed depends partly on the age of the person claiming the relief and partly on how long he has owned the business asset. The maximum amount of relief that can be claimed is £50,000 and that can be claimed by someone who is sixty-five and who has owned the business for ten years. The amount of the relief is reduced by £10,000 for each complete year below sixty-five (or a proportion if less than a year) and no exemption is available before the age of sixty. If the business has been owned for less than ten years then the amount of the relief is (further) reduced by 10% for each year less than ten years. Thus, for a sixty-two year old person who has owned the business for eight years the relief will be £50,000 reduced to £20,000 because of his age; and that £20,000 will be further reduced to £16,000 because the business has not been owned for the full ten years.

The relieved gains are those, up to the stated limits, on chargeable business assets which include those used in the trade or profession including goodwill, but which exclude those held as investments and those on the disposal of which no chargeable gain accrues. This relief is important to remember when considering the problems of retiring from a continuing firm (see p 155).

Gift of business assets (s 126). Where an individual disposes of, otherwise than at arm's length, assets used in the donor's business or shares in his family trading company to a person (which includes disposals to companies), then any capital gain may be held over if the donor and donee jointly elect. Any retirement relief is taken first; the balance of the gain then being held over.

Gifts (Finance Act 1980, s 79). A new relief was introduced for gifts of any assets, where the disposal is made to an individual. Where the relief applies, there will be no charge to CGT until the transferee sells the asset. The relief has to be claimed by both transferor and transferee, and the gain is held over until the final sale. Again any retirement relief is calculated first in determining the gain to be held over. This relief has, because of its general application, largely replaced the relief for gifts of business assets which now only applies to disposals to companies. Here is an example of the reliefs as they apply to a businessman who is retiring.

Example:
A starts a business in 1975 aged fifty-six. He has two shops valued at £15,000 and £12,000, and the goodwill of the business is valued at £15,000. In 1977 he sells shop no 2 for £17,000 and buys a new one for £18,000. In 1982 he passes the business to his son. It is now valued at £100,000—the shops being worth £50,000 and the goodwill being worth £50,000. *A* is sixty-three. The gain on the sale of shop no 2 in 1972 has been rolled over, and so in 1982 the capital gain on the shops is £22,000 (work it out), and

the gain on goodwill is £35,000 making a total gain of £57,000. Retirement relief is available.

A owned the business for seven years and is sixty-three, so he can claim 7/10ths of £30,000, ie £21,000. Thus on giving the business to his son there is a chargeable gain of £36,000. However, by virtue of s 79 of the Finance Act 1980 this gain is with his son's consent held over, and no CGT will be payable until the son sells the business. When he does sell the business, the acquisition cost will be taken to be £100,000–£36,000 (the gain held over) = £64,000. If he in turn passes the business to his son, or daughter, the same reliefs will apply.

Other reliefs. There are also reliefs which apply to gains made by charities, or on disposals to charities, and reliefs which apply to works of art and historic houses.

5 Capital transfer tax

Capital transfer tax (CTT) (introduced by the Finance Act 1975) is charged on all lifetime transfers of property; it is also charged on all property in a person's estate at the date of death. There are, however, certain exemptions and reliefs. Where lifetime transfers are concerned it is a tax levied on gifts. It is charged whenever the transferor's estate diminishes in value as a result of the gift.

To be exact CTT is a charge on the value transferred by a chargeable transfer which is any transfer of value made by an individual after 26 March 1974. A transfer of value is defined as 'any disposition made by a person . . . as a result of which the value of his estate immediately after the disposition is less than it would be but for the disposition'. Thus as with CGT, where there has to be a disposal before tax can be charged, here there has to be a disposition. Disposition is not precisely defined. The word includes failure to pursue a claim against another, failure to exercise a right by which the estate of the person so failing diminishes (ie does not increase) in value. It will include interest-free loans, because the lender's estate has diminished (ie has not increased) to the extent of the interest forgone. A person's estate is defined as 'the aggregate of all the property to which he is beneficially entitled, except that the estate of a person immediately before his death does not include excluded property'. Thus, eg, property held by him as a trustee does not form part of his estate.

If property is sold for its market value there can be no CTT because there has been no diminution in the value of his estate; there may of course be liability to CGT as there may also be on a gift of that property. Section 20(4) of the Finance Act 1975 provides that a disposition is not a transfer of value if it is shown that it was not intended, and was not made in a transaction intended, to confer any gratuitous benefit on any person and either: (*a*) it was made in a transaction at arm's length between persons not connected with each other, or (*b*) that it was such as might be expected to be made in a transaction at arm's length between persons not connected with each other. Thus if property is sold at less than its market value, CTT may be charged as the transferor's estate will have diminished by the amount by which the sale price was less than market value, eg if he sells an asset worth £25,000 to his sister for £10,000, then he has effectively given her £15,000. If, however, he did not intend to confer a gratuitous benefit on anyone (a subjective test) and the other (objective) tests are satisfied there will be no charge to CTT. The definition of connected person is that in CGTA 1979, s 63 and includes spouse, relative, partner or spouse or relative of that partner. This section will be considered in greater detail when CTT and partnerships are examined in Part II of this book.

On death, tax is charged as if immediately before death a transfer of value had been made—the value transferred being equal to the value of his estate immediately before death. The value of the estate is the price it would fetch on the open market. It includes policies of insurance if the deceased was entitled to sums payable thereunder, purchased annuities continuing after the deceased's death (although there are special rules relating to annuities continuing after death under approved retirement annuity schemes) and the share of a deceased partner in partnership property.

(a) The calculation of tax

To establish the value of the transfer the transferor's estate has to be looked at immediately before and immediately after the disposition; the difference between the two values is the amount which is brought into the charge to CTT. In addition tax (not CGT) and any other costs arising on the disposition will be taken into account because they will also diminish the value of the estate.

CTT is charged according to rates laid down by statute. The present rates are contained in the Finance Act 1982. There is a higher rate of tax payable on transfers made on death or at any time within three years of death. The first £55,000 is charged at a nil rate; thereafter the tax gradually increases from 30% between £55,000 and £75,000 to 75% on transfers of £2,500,000 or more. Lower rates of tax apply where other lifetime transfers are made.

Thus the rate of tax for transfers between £55,000 and £75,000 is 15% and the top rate is 50%. CTT is calculated on a cumulative basis, not on each separate transfer. It thus applies increasingly throughout a person's life and on his death, to any transfers he makes. However, under s 43(1) of the Finance Act 1981, after ten years any gift drops out of cumulation. If therefore *A* were to make a gift of £55,000 in 1982, this at present would attract no CTT. If no further gifts were made until 1992, the £55,000 would drop out of the cumulative total, leaving it open for *A* to make a further gift of £55,000 (at present rates) with no CTT liability. Only transfers made in the ten-year period ending with the date of the transfer are thus taken into account.

In calculating the amount transferred during a person's lifetime, each gift will have to be grossed up to take account of the tax payable, unless the transferee is paying the tax. As explained before, this is because the transferor's estate diminishes in value not only to the extent of the gift but also to the extent of the tax that has to be paid; CTT by its cumulative nature is therefore a tax upon a tax in these cases.

When valuing the property transferred s 38(1) of the Finance Act 1975 provides that the value shall be the price which the property might reasonably be expected to fetch if sold on the open market at that time. There are, however, special rules that relate to the valuation of the transfer in certain cases, eg where the grant of an option excludes or restricts the right to dispose of property and the property is later disposed of. These may be particularly appropriate when a partner agrees in the partnership deed that on his retirement the remaining partners shall have the option to purchase his share of the partnership assets (see p 156).

(*b*) *Exemption and reliefs*

Schedule 6 to the Act provides for exempt transfers. An exempt transfer forms no part of the CTT calculation; remember that the first £55,000 transferred is not an exempt transfer but a transfer taxed at a nil rate and therefore is relevant to the calculation of later CTT.

Transfers between spouses. These are exempt whether made during the transferor's lifetime or on death. Once spouses have been divorced this exemption does not apply.

Transfers of £3,000 or less in any one year. These are exempt. The year is calculated to 5 April and £3,000 is calculated without consideration of tax. This exemption, if not used in one year, can be carried forward for one year.

Small gifts. Up to £250 per person may be transferred in any year.

Normal expenditure out of income, etc. If the transfer was part of the normal expenditure of the transferor and it was made out of his income, and he was left with enough income to maintain his usual standard of living, then the transfer of income is an exempt transfer. Thus a parent who pays for his children's education out of income has not made a chargeable transfer. If he or she has to pay for it out of capital, then a similar exemption is provided in s 46 of the Finance Act 1975. Gifts in consideration of marriage, to charities, to political parties, for national purposes (inter alia) are also subject to certain exemptions. There is also a relief where a transfer is followed within five years or less by the death of the transferee—the amount of tax chargeable on the transferee's estate is reduced; there are also special provisions which apply to any transfers of works of art, historic buildings, etc.

Relief for business property. Where business property is transferred whether during a person's lifetime or on death, the value of the property is reduced for the purposes of calculating any liability to CTT (Finance Act 1976, s 73). The relief applies only to relevant business property which means (*a*) a business or an interest in a business, (*b*) shares or securities of a company which gave the transferor control of the company, and (*c*) land, buildings, machinery or plant which was used wholly or mainly for the purposes of a business (company or partnership). The relief provides that in (*a*) and (*b*) the value is reduced by 50%, and in (*c*) by 30% for the purposes of calculating CTT. Any other exemptions or reliefs are given after business relief. The relief cannot be claimed unless the transferor has owned the relevant business property throughout the two years immediately preceding the transfer; or it must have replaced other relevant business property which within the last five years was owned for at least two years.

Chapter 5

Dissolution of Partnership

1 Introduction

The rules as to what happens to partnership property on dissolution are laid down in the Partnership Act 1890, and are illustrated and interpreted in a number of cases. Whilst in practice it is rare for a professional partnership to be entirely dissolved it must be remembered that every time an existing partner retires, this could amount to a dissolution of the original partnership, followed by the formation of a new partnership. The formal rules of dissolution will not usually apply in these circumstances because, like many of the provisions of the Act, they can be excluded by agreement. The practical steps to be taken on the retirement of partners, and the admission of new partners are examined in some detail in Part II of this book. This chapter is concerned with the entire dissolution of the partnership.

The provisions of the Act will apply equally where the partnership is wound up at a loss (and where perhaps the partners are made bankrupt). In these circumstances the Bankruptcy Act 1914 may also be relevant.

2 Means of dissolution

Before the rules relating to the distribution of property apply, the partnership must first be terminated according to the terms of the contract between the partners. In many cases this is done by mutual consent, whether express or implied. It will be implied in a vast number of cases where for example a new partner is admitted. Here, the implied consent of the existing partners will dissolve the old firm, and immediately, by mutual consent, they will start to trade in a new partnership. Tax lawyers will see this as a continuing partnership if the partners elect to 'continue' under the provisions of s 154(2) of the Income and Corporation Taxes Act 1970 (see p 142). Other ways of terminating the contract between the partners are laid down in ss 32–35 of the Partnership Act.

(*a*) *By expiration or notice (s 32)*

Where the partnership is entered into for a fixed term, the expiry of that term will automatically dissolve the partnership. If, as often happens in this situation, the partners continue to treat each other as partners after the technical dissolution, s 27 of the Act provides that the rights and duties of the partners remain the same as they were at the expiration of the term, but only in so far as they are consistent with a partnership at will. Thus in *Stekel* v *Ellice* [1973] 1 WLR 191 *E* was taken on as a salaried partner by *S* for a period of six months only, and was paid a specific salary. At the expiration of six months the parties continued for a further sixteen months on the same terms as before. When the contract was terminated by mutual consent *E* claimed, under s 24 of the Partnership Act, for an equal share of the profits from the date of the expiration of the fixed term, until the termination of the contract. It was held that s 27 of the Act applied and that the rights of the partners remained the same as they were at the end of the fixed term. If the partnership was not entered into for a fixed term, nor for a single adventure, it is a partnership at will, and can be ended by notice given by any partner to his fellow partners. Section 32 of the Act provides that where notice to dissolve is given, it is effective from the date of dissolution as stipulated in the notice, or, if no date is given, the date when the notice is communicated. Further by s 26(2) the notice must be in writing if the partnership is by deed; otherwise there is nothing in the Act which stipulates that the notice must be in writing.

(*b*) *By bankruptcy, death or charge (s 33)*

Unless the provisions of the section have been excluded by agreement, on the bankruptcy or death of any partner the partnership is automatically dissolved. Further if a partner allows his share of the partnership assets to be charged, then, at the option of the other partners, the partnership can be dissolved.

(*c*) *By illegality (s 34)*

In the event of a partnership subsequently becoming illegal, the association will be dissolved. For example, if a solicitor in partnership is subsequently struck off the Roll by the Disciplinary Tribunal, the partnership will automatically be dissolved; s 20 of the Solicitors Act 1974 provides that it is illegal for a solicitor to be in partnership with an unqualified person. Section 1 of the same Act provides *inter alia* that a qualified solicitor is one who holds a current practising certificate. Thus in *Hudgell Yeates & Co* v *Watson* [1978] 2 WLR 661 a partner who had failed to renew his practising certificate rendered the partnership illegal under s 34 of the Partnership Act and the partnership was automatically dissolved, despite the fact that the partners (including the defaulting partner) were unaware of the illegality. The partners' knowledge was irrelevant to s 34. The section will also apply where the object of the partnership becomes unlawful.

(d) By the court (s 35)

The court is given power to dissolve a partnership in certain circumstances. These, of course, will apply if the partnership is one for a fixed term, or when it is entered into for a specific undertaking, and a partner wishes to dissolve before the end of the period, or the completion of the undertaking. The grounds for dissolution as laid down by s 35 are:

1 A partner becomes permanently incapable of performing his part of the contract.
2 A partner has been guilty of conduct prejudicial to the business.
3 A partner has wilfully and persistently committed a breach of the partnership agreement.
4 The partnership can only be carried on at a loss.
5 The court considers it just and equitable to dissolve the partnership.

It should be noted that grounds 1–3 cannot be relied upon if the partner who is suing is the partner who is incapable or guilty of misconduct or breach. Further, by the Mental Health Act 1959 a court can order the dissolution of the partnership if, by reason of a partner's mental disorder, he is incapable of managing his affairs. Thus mental illness of a partner does not automatically dissolve a partnership. In such circumstances it is desirable for the other partners to seek an injunction preventing the mentally ill partner from interfering with the conduct of the partnership business.

3 Effect of dissolution

Once the contract between the partners has been effectively terminated, the provisions of the Act deal with the effect of dissolution.

(*a*) *Realisation of partnership assets*

On the dissolution of the partnership the assets of the partnership may be realised, and the outside creditors of the firm fully paid. Section 39 of the Act provides that each partner on dissolution shall have the right to insist that the assets of the partnership be used to pay outside creditors fully, and thereafter the surplus should be paid to the partners according to their entitlement (as to which see s 44: see p 54). To enforce this right each partner has a lien over partnership assets, such lien arising only on dissolution of the partnership. The right can be enforced by application to the Chancery Division.

(b) Partnership property

The first question a partner seeking to enforce this right must ask himself is 'What amounts to partnership assets?' The answer is to be found partly in the Act, and partly in case law.

The statutory definition of partnership property is found in ss 20 and 21 of the Act. Section 20 provides that all property and interests in property originally brought into partnership stock, or acquired on account of the firm, or for the purposes and in the course of the partnership business is partnership property. Further, by s 21, property bought with money belonging to the firm is deemed to have been bought on account of the firm. Like many of the provisions of the Act, these sections can be excluded by showing a contrary agreement. The importance of property being described as partnership property, as distinguished from that property which merely belongs to the partners as individuals, is as follows.

First, if there is an appreciation in the value of partnership property, this accrues to all the partners in accordance with their asset–surplus sharing ratio; if the property belongs to an individual partner, he alone will be entitled to the benefit of the increase. The same principle will apply to depreciation in the value of the asset. Secondly, if on dissolution, all the partners are insolvent, then by s 33 of the Bankruptcy Act 1914 the firm's creditors must first prove against the firm's assets, and not against the individual partner's own assets, and the individual partner's creditors must prove against the partner's own assets, not against the firm's assets. Further, by s 22 of the Partnership Act, the equitable doctrine of conversion applies to partnership real property and for all purposes this is treated as personalty.

Case law helps in deciding whether property belongs to the partnership or to the individual partner. The problems generally fall into two categories. First, when property is owned jointly by the partners, is this evidence that the property is partnership property? Section 2 of the Act (see p 5) specifically states that co-ownership does not of itself create partnership. The property will not automatically be partnership property even though it is used by the firm. The basic principle is one of intention of the partners. If necessary the courts will infer an intention from the partners' conduct. Thus in *Waterer* v *Waterer* (1873) LR 15 Eq 402 a father left by will his nursery business together with the land upon which the business was carried on to his three sons as tenants in common. Shortly before his death he contracted to purchase additional property and this purchase was completed by his sons after his death. The sons carried on the business in partnership until one of them decided to sell his share in the business to the other two. He received one price for both his share of the land and the business. On the death of one of the remaining partners, the question as to whether the land was partnership property arose. It was held that it was partnership property. This was the implied intention of the brothers, particularly since, when the brother sold his share in the business and the land, one price was paid, showing that the two were considered inseparable.

Secondly, what happens where one partner brings his own property into the partnership which is then used by the firm? If no agreement is made between the partners, then the case of *Miles* v *Clarke* [1953] 1 WLR 537 is authority for the rule that only such property as is necessary to give business efficacy to the relationship between the partners is to be treated as partnership property. *C* carried on business as a commercial photographer and owned a lease of his premises together with various fixtures and fittings of a photographic nature. He invited *M* in as a partner. *M* brought with him his own connections, and the two worked in partnership using the premises and fixtures and fittings. On the dissolution of the firm, the court held that only the stock in trade amounted to partnership property. *C* was to keep his premises, fixtures and fittings and each partner was to keep his own connections.

If the firm has been in existence for a number of years, the connections may well amount to goodwill. Is the value of goodwill to be taken into account on dissolution? The answer is yes; in the absence of contrary agreement, goodwill must be realised. Goodwill is difficult to define (see p 9), but it is generally taken as meaning the value a purchaser will put on a business over and above the market value of the tangible assets. It is the reputation of the business stated in financial terms.

There appears to be one exception to the rule that goodwill should be realised on dissolution. If the business is of a very personal nature then it is possible to contend that the firm has no goodwill—it is the reputation of the individual partners which is important. In such a case each partner can retain whatever goodwill he himself has acquired.

(*c*) *Distribution of partnership assets*

The method laid down by the Act for distribution of the firm's assets is to be found in s 44. This section provides that once the assets have been realised then the first to be paid are the outside creditors of the firm. Following this, each partner is to be paid rateably what is due to him from the firm as advances or loans as distinguished from capital, and then each partner is paid rateably the amount of capital due to him. If there is any surplus left after these payments, such surplus is to be paid to the partners according to their profit-sharing ratio.

However, in many cases there may be insufficent assets to pay both the outside creditors and the partners' entitlement. If this is the case the Act provides that if necessary the partners must make a payment to swell the assets of the firm in the same proportion that they were entitled to share profits.

Example:
Ash, Tray & Co is dissolved owing outside creditors a total of £43,000. The assets of the firm realise £50,000. The three partners share profits equally and their capital contributions were *A*—£10,000, *B*—£5,000 and *C*—£1,000. There are no other sums owing to the partners. The total sum due to outside creditors and partners is thus £59,000, which means that the assets are deficient by £9,000. Thus the partners need to swell the assets by this sum making a payment in the same proportion as they shared profits, ie £3,000 each. In practice *A* is owed £10,000 and must pay £3,000, so receives £7,000 net. *B* is owed £5,000, must pay £3,000 and receives £2,000 net. *C* is owed £1,000 and must pay £3,000, thus he must make a net payment to the assets of £2,000.

In the event of a partner not being able to make such a payment to swell the assets (because for example he is bankrupt) there is no provision in the Partnership Act requiring the other partners to contribute further. Thus since there will be insufficient funds to repay all the partners' entitlement to capital, such repayments must be made rateably. The authority for this is the case of *Garner* v *Murray* [1904] 1 Ch 57. Although, therefore, the general rule is that partners bear losses in the same ratio as they share profits, in this particular situation their loss is borne in the same ratio as they contributed capital.

It should be noted that whilst capital and advances are repaid to the partners on dissolution according to their entitlement, a premium paid by an incoming partner is not generally repayable on the dissolution of the firm. There are two exceptions to this rule, however. The first is where a partnership is entered into for a fixed term, but is dissolved before the end of that term. In this event, if a partner has paid a premium then by s 40 the court can order a return of the premium, or a proportionate part thereof unless the dissolution is due to the death of a partner, the misconduct of the partner who paid the premium or the partnership has been dissolved by an agreement which contained no provision for the return of the premium. The second instance when a premium (and indeed any payment made by the incoming partner) is repayable is when the partnership is dissolved for fraud or misrepresentation. In addition to any rights that the deceived partner may have under the Misrepresentation Act 1967, the Partnership Act, s 41, gives him the right to a lien over the surplus partnership assets for any sum of money paid by him for the purchase of a share, or his capital contributions; to be subrogated to (ie to stand in the place of) the creditors of the firm whom he had paid; and to be indemnified by the partner guilty of fraud or making the representation against all the debts of the firm.

Finally, on the question of the costs of winding up the partnership (a matter dear to the hearts of lawyers assisting in the dissolution) there is authority (*Potter* v *Jackson* (1880) 13 Ch D 845; *Ross* v *White* [1894] 3 Ch 326) to the effect that the costs must be paid out of the assets of the partnership after the outside creditors and the partners' advances have been paid, but before the partners are repaid their capital contributions. This means that if a partner has overdrawn his entitlement he must repay the sum of capital withdrawn in order that the assets available for the payment of costs may be ascertained.

Part II

Professional Partnerships

with special reference to solicitors' partnerships

Chapter 6

Practical Steps on Commencement

1 Finance

The financing of a partnership which is to be formed from scratch can be a complicated exercise, but it is an exercise which should be carefully completed, not only for the peace of mind of the potential partners, but also to show any lender of money that the partners fully understand the responsibilities involved. The starting point should always be a detailed estimate of the first five years' income and this should be divided into bills delivered and cash received.

Assuming two individuals *X* and *Y* are setting up as solicitors in partnership it would be necessary for them to estimate (on the basis of known connections brought into the firm) the amount of conveyancing, contentious and say probate work which would be done during the first five years. This estimate will assume that the fees will increase in subsequent years from connections made during the course of earlier years and naturally from the prevailing inflationary economic climate. From the resultant figures, the amount of cash received in each year can be estimated on the basis of say 65% of the bills delivered in the first year and 65% of the bills delivered in the second year with the addition of, in this second year, say 30% of the first year's bills. This will leave a provision for bad and doubtful debts of 5% per annum of bills delivered.

In later years, assuming a sufficient inflow of work, the estimates can be obtained from using a simple time-costing system; that is during those later years, assuming that each partner is able to work for 1,100 chargeable hours a year, a figure can be ascertained which will give the partners an hourly charging rate which will allow the expenses and overheads to be paid, and a suitable standard of living to be achieved. (As to time-costing systems generally, see p 113.) The number of hours is based on the supposition that a 35-hour week will generate 1,820 hours, and that only 60% of this time is directly chargeable to clients; the remaining 40% being taken up in administrative business, holidays, etc.

Once an estimated figure for income has been found, the potential partners should then estimate the outgoings and expenses of the business over the five year period. These should be divided into expenditure of a revenue type (for example, rent, rates, typing, wages, light and heat, etc) and expenditure of a capital nature (for example, office equipment, furniture, library, etc). Again in the second and subsequent years the revenue expenditure will increase both as a result of increased work and inflation; the capital expenditure should only increase in those subsequent years in respect of additional equipment required—increases in the library stocks, for example. Other expenditure such as money required to be expended on clients' disbursements should also be noted, and sums included for national insurance contributions and, in the later years, a provision for income tax.

Example:

Income

Year	*Bills delivered* £	*Cash received* £	
1	6,000	3,900	
2	13,000	10,250	(30% of year 1 65% of year 2)
3	20,000	16,900	(30% of year 2 65% of year 3)
4	30,000	25,500	(30% of year 3 65% of year 4)
5	38,000	33,700	(30% of year 4 65% of year 5)

Expenditure

Year	*Revenue expenses* £	*Capital expenses* £	*Unpaid disbursements* £	*Increase* £
1	5,500	3,000	450	—
2	7,200	750	800	350
3	9,500	900	1,200	400
4	14,200	1,000	1,800	600
5	16,000	1,100	2,500	700

Final Results

	Year 1	*Year 2*	*Year 3*	*Year 4*	*Year 5*
	£	£	£	£	£
Revenue expenses	5,500	7,200	9,500	14,200	16,000
Capital expenses	3,000	750	900	1,000	1,100
Increased unpaid disbursements	450	350	400	600	700
National insurance	400	400	400	400	400
Income tax	—	—	—	900	1,300
	9,350	8,700	11,200	17,100	19,500
Less cash received	3,900	10,250	16,900	25,500	33,700
Net inflow	(5,450)	1,550	5,700	8,400	14,200
Less loan interest (20% pa)	1,100	1,100	1,100	1,100	1,100
Distributable income	(6,550)	450	4,600	7,300	13,100

The final results of the estimated income and expenditure can now be drawn up showing at the end of each year the net expected deficit or income.

This example clearly shows conservative estimates, and it means that in order to finance this partnership the sum of approximately £6,500 (the deficit in the first year) is required. This means borrowing this sum, on the assumption that the partners are unable to find it from their own resources. In addition to this sum, the partners must live for the first year, and supplement their income in subsequent years. As to the £6,500, this can be borrowed in the name of the partnership, meaning that both partners are jointly liable for repayment (see s 9 of the Partnership Act, p 14). By borrowing this sum, the interest payable will be a deductible expense of the firm for income tax purposes (see p 140).

As to the further sum required for living purposes, the partners may well decide that their best course is to make their own arrangements, as opposed to arrangements made through the firm. The individual needs of each partner will be different, depending upon a number of matters, ranging from style of living to spouse's income. Further, it is unlikely that each partner would wish to be liable for the debts of the other, this being the position if the sum borrowed for living purposes was borrowed in the name of the firm. Consequently in later years when the partnership was providing an income for the partners, it would make more sense to repay the personal loans first (since the interest on these would not be deductible for tax purposes) and only later seek to repay the partnership loan, making full use during the early years of the interest as a tax deduction.

Having decided upon the amount of money required, the next step is to negotiate a loan on the most favourable terms. In the case of a firm of solicitors, the best place to open negotiations would be one of the larger clearing banks. Since the very nature of a solicitor's business will ultimately involve large sums of money being deposited in a client bank account, this is a useful incentive to a bank manager to offer favourable terms on the loan. The options open to the bank range from a fixed term loan (which may be anything up to fifteen years) to an extended overdraft facility. In either case the banks are usually going to look for a 50% stake in the business by the applicants. Certainly no bank is going to provide 100% finance. The bank will also look for some security for its money, and this can be provided either by each individual granting the bank a mortgage over their respective houses, or providing some life insurance policy as security. There are some schemes linked with life assurance companies whereby the capital amount of the loan is repaid on the maturity of an endowment policy, and in the meantime the individual pays interest only to the bank. The policy in these circumstances is clearly going to be assigned to the bank.

The amount of interest paid can also differ according to the scheme negotiated. In some circumstances interest will be variable and linked to the bank's base rate. (Professional partnerships sometimes have the edge over other partnerships and whilst the normal rate is 3–5% above base rate, it may be possible to negotiate interest at 2–2½% above base rate.) Other loans will be fixed rate interest, and whilst these are usually more expensive, they can have advantages if negotiated in times where the prevailing interest rate is low.

The above principles of finance will apply equally to those potential partners intending to join an existing firm. In these circumstances, however, the loan is likely to be for a capital contribution to the firm (for which the partner will get full tax relief on the interest payable) and there is unlikely to be any further loan required for living expenses. The partner might however consider other means of contributing towards his capital. For example, if his fellow partners agree, it would be cheaper for him to contribute a specified amount each year from undrawn profits until he reaches the required level of capital.

2 Commencement date

The actual date of commencement needs careful consideration for a number of reasons. If a new partnership is being formed there are advantages in being able to pick a commencement date which is not only convenient but which will also save the partners money, or potentially earn them more money. A date which saves money can be ascertained by reference to the basis of assessment for income tax purposes. Tax, as we have seen, is payable on a preceding year basis (apart from the special rules relating to the opening and closing years of a partnership). Consequently there is a delay between earning the profits and the payment of the tax on those profits. The tax is payable by reference to the firm's accounting periods. Therefore by choosing a commencement date the firm's accounting period can be settled which will give the maximum delay between earning and paying tax.

Example 1:
AB & Co commence business on 1 April and their accounting period is twelve months to 31 March each year.

Profits made in the accounting year 1 April 1980–31 March 1981 will be taxed in the year of assessment 1981/82. Since the tax must be paid in two instalments on (in this example) 1 January 1982 and 1 July 1982, there is a delay of up to fifteen months from the end of the accounting period to the last instalment.

Example 2:
CD & Co commence business on 11 April and their accounting period is twelve months to 10 April each year.

Profits made in the accounting year 11 April 1980–10 April 1981 will be taxed in the year of assessment 1982/83. Since the tax is payable in two instalments on 1 January 1983 and 1 July 1983 there is a delay of almost twenty-seven months from the end of the accounting period to the last instalment.

The advantages of choosing the commencement date in *2* above are obvious.

One important word of warning must be given. The main advantages of the preceding year basis will be found when profits are rising in each year. If profits are falling, it will mean that the tax must be paid in the current year on higher profits made in the preceding year. The importance of a tax reserve cannot be overestimated. An amount equal to the sum ultimately due in tax should be set aside each year to meet the tax demand as and when it arrives. This sum can be put in short term securities and so earn interest for the partnership (see p 103).

The second reason why a commencement date needs careful consideration is in relation to advertising. For many professional partnerships advertising causes no difficulties—once the business has commenced, the firm can freely advertise in the press. However some professions (notably solicitors) have hard-and-fast rules on advertising. It is important that such firms take every permissible step to make the public aware of their existence. This means timing the commencement date so that the firm's name appears in both the local telecom telephone directory and the 'Yellow Pages'; further, as far as solicitors are concerned, ensuring that the firm's name appears in the next edition of the *Law List* (now published annually as part of *The Solicitors' Diary*).

3 Insurance

It goes without saying that the newly formed partnership should insure all the assets of the partnership and the buildings. A standard policy can be issued in respect of buildings and contents. Further, a professional partnership which by its very nature involves the posting and receipt of valuable documents should consider insuring contents of letters and parcels. This means that if a valuable document is lost in the post, the partnership will not have to rely upon compensation being paid by the Post Office. In addition, solicitors should consider other insurances. If the firm has a conveyancing department insurance policies are available to ensure that all properties where a solicitor is acting for the purchaser are insured for their market value on exchange of contracts. This is clearly a short-term measure and permanent insurance will have to be taken out by either the purchaser or his building society. However, it will cover the period between exchange of contracts and completion.

By far the most important insurance which needs to be taken out is insurance cover against professional negligence. Since 1975 it has been compulsory for all solicitors who are, or who are held out to the public as, principals in private practice to have this insurance. By the Solicitors' Indemnity Rules 1975–1981 the Law Society maintains a master policy of insurance and arranges for all solicitors to whom these rules apply to be issued with a certificate of insurance in the form set out in the master policy. In order that solicitors do comply with these rules they must produce evidence (in the form of a tear-off slip) of the insurance to the Law Society when they apply for their annual practising certificate. Since the insurance runs from 1 September each year until 31 August in the following year, and the practising certificate must be applied for on or before 1 November each year, there is ample time for a solicitor to comply with these regulations.

An annual premium (or a proportionate part thereof) is payable. The current premiums are (1981–82) £1,033 pa for solicitors practising within the inner London area and £833 pa for all other solicitors. This premium is payable by the sole practitioner, or in the case of a partnership, by each partner. There are lower premiums for low fee earners (ie those solicitors whose gross fees do not exceed £10,000 in a year). Proposals have been made to change the basis upon which premiums are paid. The change, if implemented, will mean that premiums will be assessed on the gross fees earned by solicitors rather than, as at present, fixed premiums (see Solicitors' Indemnity (Gross Fees) Rules 1981). There are no provisions for 'no-claim bonus' but with effect from 1 September 1980 those firms with high claims records can have their premiums 'loaded' by the insurers. The amount of cover afforded by the master cover is £60,000 per claim in respect of sole practitioners, and £50,000 per claim per partner in respect of partnerships. Clearly in many firms this is inadequate and topping up cover can either by obtained through the scheme or on the open market.

4 Registration

The partnership may require to be registered for Value Added Tax purposes. Even if the firm is not required to be so registered, it may wish to register voluntarily. VAT is charged under s 2 of the Finance Act 1972 on the supply of goods or services where the supply is a taxable supply and is made by a taxable person in the course or furtherance of a business carried on by him.

Under the Finance Act 1982 persons or firms who make taxable supplies of broadly £17,000 or more pa (or £6,000 per quarter) must be registered for VAT purposes. The advantages of being registered even where the taxable supplies do not exceed £17,000 are that any VAT paid by the firm (input tax) is reclaimable by the firm. Registration is effected by using forms VAT 1 and VAT 2.

Solicitors require a further form of registration in that they must have in force a current practising certificate issued by the Law Society before they are able to practise. Practising certificates fall due for renewal on 1 November each year and the current fee (1981–82) is £60. In addition to this fee solicitors are required to pay a further sum to the compensation fund (currently, 1981–82, £40). This fund is administered by the Law Society and is used to make payments to clients of solicitors who have suffered financial loss as a result of their solicitor's dishonesty. The payments are made at the discretion of the Council of the Law Society. It should be noted that the fund does not exist to pay clients who have suffered loss through mere negligence. In these circumstances indemnity insurance may assist the client.

5 Notification

If the partnership is to employ staff, the wages of the employees will be paid net of income tax on the Pay As You Earn basis. It will therefore be necessary to notify the local tax office of the commencement of the business in order that a monthly cheque for PAYE deductions can be sent to the Revenue.

The local Department of Health and Social Security will also have to be notified in respect of national insurance deductions from employees' wages and also self-employed contributions from the partners.

In a solicitors' partnership it is also possible to notify the public of the existence of the firm as a result of a slight relaxation of the rules relating to advertising. The basic rule in respect of advertising as far as solicitors are concerned is to be found in r 1 of The Solicitors' Practice Rules 1936–1972. This provides that:

> A solicitor shall not obtain or attempt to obtain professional business by . . . doing or permitting to be done without reasonable justification anything which by its manner, frequency or otherwise advertises his practice as a solicitor.

The relaxation of the rules referred to above now means that a solicitor can notify the public of the commencement of a new firm and the opening of a new office by notices in the local and national press. The notices must be in a prescribed form with regard to size, and must not appear to amount to advertising, but merely be a notification. Up to three notices can be inserted in both the local and national newspapers, during the month following the commencement. It is also usual and permissible for solicitors to notify fellow professional members by inserting notices in the legal press.

6 Licence

The only licence which may be required by a professional partnership is a licence granted by the Director General of Fair Trading under the provisions of the Consumer Credit Act 1974. Whilst at the time of writing many of the provisions of the Act are not in force, the licensing provisions are. Broadly if the partnership wishes to engage in any consumer credit business it will require a licence under the Act. Many professional partnerships will require such a licence because of the wide definition of consumer credit. Whilst solicitors are exempt from the provisions in respect of credit in the course of acting in contentious work (s 146 of the 1974 Act), they and other professions will require a licence if they act as credit brokers (ie introduce clients to persons who give or arrange credit), debt collectors or merely if they lend money to clients.

There are two types of licence which can be granted by the Director General. The first is a standard licence which specifies a named person and the type of business he is entitled to carry on. The second is a group licence which will permit a specified group of persons to carry out the type of business specified in the licence. A group licence was issued to the solicitors' profession and was renewed for a period of ten years from 1979. Group licences have also been issued to accountants, but other professional partnerships will be required to apply individually to the Director General for a standard licence. Failure to obtain the licence makes any regulated consumer credit agreement unenforceable by the partnership unless the Director General orders otherwise.

Chapter 7

Partnership Articles

1 Introduction

In the previous chapter we looked at a number of practical steps which should be taken before the commencement of the partnership. One extremely important step which must be added to this list is the consideration of the terms and drafting of the partnership articles considered in this chapter. A specimen partnership deed is set out in Appendix 3.

There is in law no obligation upon the partners to set out the terms of the partnership agreement in writing, and equally, if the agreement is in writing there is no obligation that it should be under seal. In cases where there is no written evidence of the existence of a partnership, the terms of the oral agreement can be proved by parol evidence or from the course of dealings between the partners, and in the absence of an oral contrary agreement the various provisions of the Partnership Act 1890 will apply to the relationship. There is, however, one exception to this rule. Where the agreement between the partners includes an agreement for the transfer of land the provisions of s 40 of the Law of Property Act 1925 must be complied with. The case of *Gray* v *Smith* (1889) 43 Ch D 208 is authority for the proposition that whilst a partnership in land may be proved by parol evidence, an agreement dealing with land as part of the partnership assets must be evidenced by a sufficient memorandum in writing under the Law of Property Act 1925 to be enforceable. Thus if the agreement provides that as a part of his capital contribution a partner should bring in freehold land as partnership property, this agreement should be evidenced in writing (or it will not become partnership property).

It would be imprudent for any partner to rely upon oral evidence of the existence of any agreement with his fellow partners. Disputes and difficulties may more easily arise if the exact terms of the agreement are not settled and recorded in writing for the avoidance of doubt (see the leading case of *Miles* v *Clarke* [1953] 1 WLR 537). Consequently it is usual for all the important terms of an agreement to be embodied in a written partnership agreement or articles. These may either be in the form of a mutual agreement where the consideration consists of the mutual obligations and benefits conferred by the agreement, or in the form of a deed by way of mutual covenant. The only legal implication of having the agreement embodied in a deed is that by s 26(2) of the Partnership Act where there is a partnership at will, capable of being terminated by notice (see p 50) then 'a notice in writing, signed by the partner giving it, shall be sufficient for this purpose'. There is no requirement for such notice to be in writing if the partnership agreement is not under seal.

The articles should set out the objects of the firm so that there can be no doubt in the future as to why the partnership was formed. This aspect is the closest that partners get to having a memorandum of association with an objects clause required by all incorporated bodies under the Companies Act 1948–81. However there are differences between the objects clause of a partnership agreement and that included in a company's memorandum of association.

First, the partnership can change its objects freely provided all the partners agree to such change. Section 19 of the Act provides:

> The mutual rights and duties of partners, whether ascertained by agreement or defined by this Act, may be varied by the consent of all the partners, and such consent may be either express or implied from a course of dealings.

Even where the original agreement is in writing the partners may, either orally or by a course of dealings, vary that agreement. Thus this is an exception to the general rule that a written agreement cannot be varied by parol evidence only. Secondly, the objects of a partnership are not public documents nor need they be made available to the public for inspection at any registry. The difficulties which have arisen in company law from the ultra vires doctrine have not generally affected partnerships. The simplicity with which the partners may change their objects by a course of dealings means that there is no question of a partnership contract proving ultra vires and therefore void provided all the partners have agreed to that change. On the other side of the coin, outsiders dealing with individual partners have no constructive knowledge of the objects of the partnership nor have they any knowledge of the rest of the contents of the articles relating to the restriction of an individual partner's authority to bind the firm other than that which they can discover from their own observation and enquiry. Both these points may be relevant when advising on the question of contracts with outsiders by reference to s 5 of the Partnership Act (see p 11).

In addition to the objects, the deed should regulate the rights of the partners amongst themselves, and this can be done by setting out certain particular rights and obligations as well as excluding or modifying certain rights and duties which otherwise would be implied by the Partnership Act. It is clearly impossible for every potential problem area to be singled out and included in the deed; certain matters must be left out, and the regulation of them left to general law. However, when drafting articles of partnership major points of possible potential difficulty should be grasped and included in the agreement for both clarity and future reference. With this in mind, the following matters should appear in the partnership agreement.

2 Partners' names

Capacity to enter into a partnership is generally co-extensive with capacity to contract. Hence any person with such capacity can enter into a partnership agreement, and this will include an incorporated body provided that its objects clause, contained in the memorandum of association, permits such a relationship. Exceptions to the general rule include enemy aliens (*R* v *Kupfer* [1915] 2 KB 321) and, it appears, a clerk in Holy Orders holding an ecclesiastical preferment (Pluralities Act 1838, s 29).

Minors can validly enter into a partnership agreement, but can repudiate it before or within a reasonable time of attaining their majority at the age of eighteen. If a minor validly repudiates the contract of partnership he can recover money paid by him under the provisions of the contract, but only if he is able to show a complete failure of consideration (*Steinberg* v *Scala (Leeds) Ltd* [1923] 2 Ch 452, where there was consideration and no money was therefore returnable). A minor is a dangerous person for an adult to be in partnership with. He is not liable for the partnership debts and obligations incurred during his minority unless they are otherwise at law enforceable against him. Thus, to enforce such debts against the minor, an outside creditor of the firm would need to show that the contract with the firm (and thus the minor) was for 'necessaries'; this onus of proof would in most cases be impossible to discharge. The adult partners would, however, be fully liable for those debts and obligations although it was suggested by Lord Herschell in *Lovell and Christmas* v *Beauchamp* [1894] AC 607 that in these circumstances the adult partner may be able to insist that the partnership assets be used to pay the creditors of the firm, which would deplete the minor partner's share in the assets. In the event of a minor partner's failure to repudiate his contract within a reasonable time of attaining his majority, he will not retrospectively become liable for those partnership debts and obligations incurred during his minority, but he will, of course, be liable for such debts and obligations incurred after the attainment of his majority. The problems relating to minors in partnership will generally be of no concern in professional partnerships.

A number of professional partnerships have by statute restrictions on the capacity of members, requiring partners to be members of the profession concerned. Thus dentists and veterinary surgeons may only practise in partnership with likewise qualified professional persons. Medical doctors are different. There is no restriction in law preventing non-registered medical practitioners from practising medicine, the only restriction being that, under the Medical Act 1956, s 31, such non-registered persons are not permitted to call themselves by a number of medical titles, including physician, doctor of medicine or surgeon. There is also a restriction on setting up a professional partnership for solicitors. Under a mixture of authorities including the Solicitors Act 1974 and Practice Rules issued by the Law Society (and binding upon the profession) solicitors are not permitted to enter into partnership to carry on the profession of a solicitor with an unqualified person. In order to safeguard the independence of the profession, r 3 of the Solicitors' Practice Rules 1936–72 provides that a solicitor may not share his professional fees with an unqualified person; this rule is supplemented by s 39 of the Solicitors Act 1974 which provides that a solicitor shall be struck off the Roll if he be proved to have permitted the use of his name for the profit of an unqualified person. A qualified solicitor is defined by s 1 of the 1974 Act as someone who has been admitted a solicitor, has his name entered on the Roll, and who has in force a current practising certificate. Even accepting that any potential partners in a solicitors' practice are qualified persons, there are further restrictions under the Solicitors' Practice Rules of 1975. These rules ensure that every office in a solicitors' practice is supervised by a qualified solicitor who has been admitted as such for at least three years. Whilst solicitors who have not been admitted for three years have the capacity to enter into a partnership it follows, as a result of the 1975 Practice Rules, that two or more solicitors not so qualified cannot themselves form a partnership.

3 Partnership name

Generally speaking there is a complete freedom of choice with regard to the name of the firm, though the last word in the firm's name must not be the word 'limited'. This is specifically provided for in s 439 of the Companies Act 1948 and the section lays down a penalty of a fine not exceeding £5 per day for breach. The use of the words 'and Co' have no special significance since by usage these words are applied to both incorporated and unincorporated associations.

Despite the fact that any name may generally be taken by the firm, there are certain consequences if the name is not the true surnames of the partners in the firm. Where the partnership name does not consist of the surnames of all partners without any addition other than their forenames or initials the firm must comply with s 29 of the Companies Act 1981. This provides that all business letters, written orders for goods or services to be supplied, invoices and receipts issued by the partnership must state in legible characters the name of each partner and an address at which service of any document relating to the partnership will be effective. Further, at all the premises where the partnership practises there must be displayed a notice containing such names and addresses.

There is an exception in respect of partnerships consisting of more than twenty partners. In this case the partnership is permitted to maintain at its principal place of business a list of the partners' names, provided the letters, etc, contain a statement as to the address of the principal office and that the partners' names are open to inspection. This will mean that the partners' names need not appear on the notepaper. If, however, one or more partners' names do appear other than in the text of the letter or as a signatory, then all the partners' names must appear.

There are penalties for failing to comply with these provisions (at present a maximum fine of £200). Non-compliance may also lead to a disability to pursue a claim made on a contract in breach of these provisions by the partnership, if the defendant can show that he has been unable to pursue a claim against the partnership because of the breach, or that he has suffered financial loss in connection with the contract, again as a result of the breach (see s 30 of the Companies Act 1981).

A further restriction on choice of name will apply if the name is likely to deceive the public into believing that it is dealing with a rival firm. In this case a passing off action will lie to restrain the use of the name. In certain circumstances this could include the names of the partners themselves if by the use of those names it is clear that the public will be misled (see for example *Croft* v *Day* (1843) 7 Beav 84). The use of a name can be restrained by injunction.

In a solicitors' partnership, the choice of name is restricted by the operation of the Solicitors' Practice Rules 1967 which provide that only the names of solicitors holding a current practising certificate may appear on the professional stationery of the firm. This rule is subject to the exception that firms may continue to practise under the name of a predecessor or former partner, or may use a name which was in use before the operation of the Rules. The practical effect of these rules is that any new firm of solicitors must take as its name the names of some or all of the partners. If they decide to use only some of their names as the firm name, then the names of all of the partners must appear on the letter heads (subject to the exception referred to above where the number of partners exceeds twenty).

4 Commencement and duration

The commencement of the partnership is a mixed question of law and fact; for there to be a partnership, the relevant acts must satisfy the requirement of s 1 of the Partnership Act, and also the partners must have started in business. This means that whilst, in most cases, the date of commencement will be stated in the written partnership agreement, this date is not conclusive evidence of the commencement. The completion of the partnership agreement will not of itself create a partnership, unless the agreement is put into immediate effect. In a number of cases it is possible for the partners to commence 'carrying on a business' within s 1 of the Act, and at a later date formalise the agreement by executing a deed. In these circumstances the date of commencement should be stated in the deed as being the earlier date, provided of course the terms of the original informal agreement between the partners constituted partnership.

If a written agreement is delayed, the partners cannot avoid the obligations of partnership by attempting to show in the written agreement that the partnership commenced only on the execution of the agreement. For example *A* and *B* informally start their business on 1 January, and *A* contracts for business goods with *T*. On 1 February a partnership deed is executed stating the commencement of the business to be the date of the deed. In these circumstances, provided the conditions of s 1 were satisfied from 1 January, *T* will be able to treat *A* and *B* as partners despite the statement in their deed, and thus render *B* liable as well as *A* for the contract price. Many of the problems which have arisen in this area relate to taxation. In *Waddington* v *O'Callaghan* (1931) 16 TC 187 a solicitor informed his son on 31 December 1928 that he intended to take him into partnership. A deed of partnership was executed, but not until 11 May 1929, expressed to have effect from the previous 1 January. It was held on the facts that the oral agreement showed clearly that there was not to be a partnership unless and until the terms of the deed of partnership were agreed between father and son. Hence the partnership created by the deed commenced on the date of the deed.

The duration of the partnership is a matter upon which any potential partners must agree. In the absence of any specific agreement, the partnership is a 'partnership at will', which means that it can be ended by the will of any of the partners. Section 26(1) of the Act states that when no fixed term has been agreed any partner can end the relationship by giving notice to all the other partners. Section 26(2) (see p 69) requires the notice to be in writing if the original partnership agreement is by deed; otherwise oral notice will suffice. Once given the notice cannot be withdrawn without the consent of all the partners (*Jones* v *Lloyd* (1874) LR 18 Eq 265). Other options are open (and are usually taken by potential partners). The drawback with partnerships at will is that whilst they allow partners to leave the partnership with ease, no notice period is required and therefore years of work may be brought to an end at the will of one partner. Reading s 26 in conjunction with s 39 (see p 52), a partner who dissolves the partnership with immediate effect has the right to insist that the partnership assets be realised, outside creditors paid off, and any surplus divided among the partners. It is therefore usual in practice to restrict the operation of s 26 by expressly including in the agreement that notice of, say, six months (or whatever period may be appropriate to the particular business) should be given to dissolve the firm and further to provide how the partners are to be paid their entitlement.

Alternatively, the partnership agreement could provide that dissolution should only take effect by mutual arrangement. In *Moss* v *Elphick* [1910] 1 KB 846 this phrase was interpreted as meaning that neither of the partners could unilaterally determine the partnership, and therefore the duration of the firm was the joint lives of the partners.

Much depends on the type of partnership and the particular partners. If an existing sole proprietor wishes to offer a partnership to a bright junior, then it may be in his interest to agree that the duration of the partnership should be for a fixed number of years, and thereafter should be determined by six months' notice in writing on either side. This way the sole proprietor can ensure that his new partner does not spend twelve months building up his own goodwill, and then leave the firm. Equally where two or more potential partners are considering starting a business from scratch, there will be difficult financial times ahead, and in order to make sure that no one deserts in the first two or three years, an initial fixed term may be considered. In other circumstances, it may be more appropriate just to provide an open-ended contract with a specified notice period on either side. In the event of a fixed term being agreed there should be provision for continuance of the firm upon the same terms as before, after the expiry of the fixed term. Whilst it is better to include this expressly in the agreement (so that partners have no doubt as to what will happen at the end of the fixed term) s 27 of the Act deals specifically with this situation. As has been shown (see p 50) where a fixed term expires and the partners continue in partnership without a new agreement, then the rights and duties of the partners remain the same as they were at the expiration of the term so far as they are consistent with a partnership at will.

5 Place of business

The principal place of business and any branch offices should be stated. If the firm has more than one place of business, the articles should state which partner is primarily responsible for the running of which office. One reason for specifying the principal place of business (if more than one) lies in s 24(9) of the Partnership Act which requires the partnership books to be kept there.

6 Partnership property

Because of the distinction between partnership and an individual's property (see p 52) and because that distinction often depends upon the intention of the parties, the importance of including in the articles a clear statement as to what is (and also what is not) partnership property cannot be over-emphasised. Quite often a partner will bring in property as part of his capital contribution and details of this should be set out in the articles. If it is the intention of a partner to transfer the freehold estate in his land to the partnership (possibly as part of his capital contribution) then the land can be specifically transferred to not more than four partners who should then declare in the articles that they hold on trust for the partnership (thus satisfying the provisions of s 53(1) of the Law of Property Act 1925). Alternatively the partner intending to transfer the land may himself make such a declaration of trust.

If, however, the partnership premises are owned by an individual partner, who allows the partnership to use the premises at a nominal or other rent, this fact should appear in the articles. In such circumstances there should also be a lease of the premises to the partnership. Care should be taken to include in the lease a provision allowing renewal on expiry of the lease. Further, if there is no specific lease for a particular term the court may infer a tenancy for the duration of the partnership (see *Pocock* v *Carter* [1912] 1 Ch 663; but compare *Rye* v *Rye* [1962] AC 496). Where an individual's own premises are themselves leasehold, and the lease includes a prohibition against assignment, the use of those premises by the partnership will not amount to a breach of such a clause (*Gian Singh & Co* v *Derray Nahar* [1965] 1 WLR 412). However, in such circumstances details of the arrangement should be set out in the partnership deed to avoid future doubt. Further the deed should include an indemnity clause whereby all the partners indemnify the lessor partner against claims for rent or breaches of other covenants contained in the lease.

7 Partnership capital

The partners should agree their capital contributions to the firm, and this should be stated in the partnership agreement. In the absence of a specific agreement s 24(1) of the Partnership Act provides that 'All the partners are entitled to share equally in the capital and profits of the business and must contribute equally towards the losses whether of capital or otherwise sustained by the firm'. Thus, if partners are going to contribute towards capital in unequal shares and expect to be repaid in unequal shares, they should state this fact in the articles. Failure to do so will not imply the statutory provision providing the partners are able to show a contrary agreement by a course of dealing (see s 19 of the Partnership Act, p 69). However, this is clearly an unsatisfactory solution, and for the sake of clarity, express provision relating to capital contributions should be set out in the partnership deed.

Capital is, of course, returnable if the partnership is dissolved in a solvent state, or in the event of one partner retiring from or otherwise leaving the partnership. Therefore in the partnership books of account there should be shown the amount of initial capital contributed by each partner. It is unusual to deal with subsequent profits through the capital accounts of the partners; the capital accounts will normally remain unaltered, until such time as the partners agree to increase the capital, or a partner starts to withdraw capital as distinct from profits. Care should be taken in drafting the partnership agreement to provide for a scheme whereby capital can be increased. Depending upon the circumstances, the partners can either agree that their unanimous consent is required before any increase, or that an increase can be effected by a majority decision. In either event it is usual to provide that such increase be effected either on a *pro rata* basis, or in the same share that they receive profits.

The partnership agreement should also provide for payment of interest on capital in certain circumstances. Section 24 of the Act, which deals with the internal affairs of the partnership, provides (*inter alia*) that in the absence of agreement all partners are entitled to share equally in the profits of the firm and that no partner is entitled to receive interest on his capital contribution. By providing interest on capital in the agreement, the partners merely adjust any profit-sharing ratio, since such payment of interest will be made, out of net profit, before the ascertainment of the partners' share of the profits. Thus if one partner has subscribed considerably more capital than another but both partners work full time for the firm, whilst they will probably agree that profits should be shared equally, it would be more equitable to allow interest on capital, which effectively adjusts the final profit-sharing ratio. It is important to realise that such a payment of interest merely amounts to a method of dividing profits between the partners, and, unlike interest payable to outsiders, it is not a deductible expense of the firm for tax purposes.

In addition to providing in the partnership agreement details of capital contributions, prudent partners will also include details of how that capital is to be repaid in the event of a partner retiring.

Example:
Three partners (*X*, *Y*, *Z*) in *XYZ & Co* have contributed capital to the firm as follows: *X*—£20,000; *Y*—£15,000; *Z*—£5,000. *X*, aged sixty-four, is retiring at the end of the next financial year. At such a time he is entitled to the return of his capital contribution. *Y* and *Z* are to continue in partnership together. If the partnership agreement is silent as to capital repayment, *X* can insist upon his full £20,000 at the date of his retirement. This may put the firm into severe financial difficulties; it might not have the cash or borrowing power to make this payment. If *X* insists on a full repayment, *Y* and *Z* might have to sell the firm's assets and thus possibly destroy the firm in order to pay *X*. Alternatively if they have the borrowing power, interest will have to be paid on the loan.

Far better in the example shown above for the partners to have agreed specifically that on death or retirement of a partner his share of capital should be repaid by instalments for example. A common clause found in professional partnerships is an agreement to pay the retiring partner an agreed first instalment (say £5,000) followed by the balance due in four equal annual instalments, together with interest thereon. With today's fluctuating interest rates it is possibly better to fix the interest rate by reference to the current base rate of the major banks. The remaining partners can then make provision for the annual repayments by, for example, ensuring that a proportion of profits is left in the firm by them.

In the absence of a specific agreement as to repayment of capital, s 42 provides that if, following the death or retirement of a partner, the firm continues to use his capital without repayment, the retired partner, or his estate, shall either be entitled to such share of the profits since his retirement which is deemed by the court to be attributable to his share, or to interest at 5% per annum.

8 Profits, drawings, outgoings and losses

Section 24 of the Partnership Act deals with the interests and duties of partners in the absence of any agreement. The relevant parts are as follows:

(1) All the partners are entitled to share equally in the capital and

profits of the business and must contribute equally towards the losses whether of capital or otherwise sustained by the firm . . .

(3) A partner making, for the purpose of the partnership, any actual payment or advance beyond the amount of capital which he has agreed to subscribe, is entitled to interest at the rate of five per cent. per annum from the date of the payment or advance.

(4) A partner is not entitled, before the ascertainment of profits, to interest on the capital subscribed by him . . .

(6) No partner shall be entitled to remuneration for acting in the partnership business . . .

Despite the fact that the Act provides for the equal share of profits, it is common to include the profit-sharing ratio in the agreement, even if this merely repeats the Act; potential partners, their advisers and indeed sometimes their potential creditors (eg a bank about to lend money to the partnership) like certainty. The reference to equal sharing of capital in s 24 is invariably excluded, both in the articles and usually by implication in the accounting procedure of the partnership, which will show separate capital accounts for each partner indicating, at any given time, their capital entitlement.

Profits for the purposes of s 24(1) mean both income and capital profits. Thus if the deed merely specifies a profit-sharing ratio, both income and capital profits (eg profits made on the sale of a fixed asset) are shared in the same ratio. If the partners wish to share income and capital profits in different ratios, they should provide for this expressly in the deed. The capital profit-sharing ratio is sometimes termed the 'asset surplus sharing ratio', and is important in the context of capital gains tax and partnerships (see p 124).

The deed should also state whether the income profits are to be ascertained on a 'cash basis', 'bills delivered basis' or 'work in progress basis'. It is usual to specify that they be ascertained in the same way in which profits for tax purposes are calculated. (For an explanation of these terms see p 116.)

Further, it is sometimes desirable to include a clause whereby profits from other connected sources are to be treated as profits of the firm. For example, a partner in a firm of solicitors may receive director's fees in respect of a directorship he holds. If he holds such a position as a result of being a partner in the firm, and attends directors' meetings in both his capacity as director and solicitor it is only fair that the fees received should be treated as part of the gross fees of the firm, and as such divided amongst the partners according to the profit-sharing ratio. (See also ss 28 and 29 of the Partnership Act, p 24.)

If a partner has advanced money to the firm, over and above his capital contribution, then before profits are assessed, interest is payable on this sum, at the rate of 5% pa (s 24(3)). Clearly, today, this rate of interest is not a commercial one, and if necessary this particular provision in s 24 should be excluded by express agreement, and a more commercial rate of interest included. As has been noted (see p 77) no interest is to be paid on a partner's capital in the firm, unless s 24(4) is excluded; in many cases it is.

Whilst no salary or other remuneration is to be paid to a partner, in practice s 24(6) is often excluded by an express agreement that such a salary be paid. Like the payment of interest on capital, this is merely a further method of adjusting the profit-sharing ratio. A large salary can be paid to the senior partner, and a scaled down salary to other partners, and thereafter the profits can be split equally. Such a salary, whilst it is deducted from the net profit before the balance is divisible between the partners equally (or in such share as they have agreed) is not a deductible expense of the firm for income tax purposes. The Revenue will treat a partner's salary as part of his share of the profit (unless he is what is known as a salaried partner when he will be paid a salary before the net profit is ascertained). The adjustment of profit by paying a salary is, however, an easy way of adjusting the profit-sharing ratio without having to split the profit into minute fractions per partner.

On his introduction a new partner may face a drop in net income, bearing in mind that he may be paying interest on a loan taken out to provide his capital contribution and may be required to leave a sum of undrawn profit in his current account and to make payments to a pension scheme. Thus a salary of a fixed sum by way of a first charge on profits can be agreed to ensure that as a minimum he receives a certain amount.

Whilst partners are entitled to the share of net profits made by the firm in accordance with either s 24 or their agreement, most firms operate on the basis of preparing annual accounts, and it is not until those accounts have been prepared and agreed that the figure available for distribution is known. Therefore some provision must be made for the payment of drawings on account of profit. Obviously such drawings are restricted by the amount of cash available at the end of each month, but it is usual to provide for a limit on the amount of drawings in the partnership agreement.

At the end of the financial year when the accounts have been agreed, the partners can settle between themselves the question of drawings. Some agreements will specifically provide that if any partner has overdrawn his entitlement then he must repay such amount to the partnership. If the agreement does not go as far as this, it will mean that an overdrawn partner will be shown in the books of the partnership as a debtor. One method of encouraging partners to keep their drawings at a minimum is to provide that interest be paid by the partners on their drawings on a day to day basis. At the end of the financial year such sums are assessed and added to the profit to be divided among the partners. Clearly this is a bookwork exercise and no sum is paid; it is a further method of adjusting the profits between the partners.

Example:
A, *B* and *C* are solicitors in partnership, each sharing profits equally. *A* is entitled to a salary of £2,000 pa and the partners' drawings for the year ended 31 December 198– amount to: *A*—£10,000; *B*—£9,000; *C*—£8,500.

It is assessed that each partner must 'pay' interest on drawings as follows: *A*—£150; *B*—£125; *C*—£115.

The net profit for the year amounts to £29,000.

The adjustments at the end of the year will be as follows:

	£
Net profit	29,000
Add interest on drawings	390
	29,390

	£
Salary *A*	2,000
Share of profit *A*(⅓)	9,130
B(⅓)	9,130
C(⅓)	9,130
	29,390

Current accounts of partners

	A	*B*	*C*
	£	£	£
Salary	2,000	—	—
Share of profit	9,130	9,130	9,130
	11,130	9,130	9,130
Less:			
Drawings	10,000	9,000	8,500
Interest on drawings	150	125	115
	980	5	515

If the partnership agreement provides for payment of salary, then it ought also to provide for the occasion where there is insufficient profit both to pay the salaries and divide the balance. In the absence of a specific clause, it is submitted that the salaries of the partners should be reduced pro rata. This may, in certain circumstances, mean that where only some partners are to receive a salary, other partners will get no share of profit.

Example:
A and *B* are entitled to salaries of £2,000 and £1,000 respectively. Thereafter profits are to be shared by all three partners, *A*, *B* and *C* equally. If the net profit in 1980 is £1,500, then dividing the salary between *A* and *B* on a pro rata basis, *A* gets £1,000 and *B* gets £500. *C* gets nothing.

In the case of *Marsh* v *Stacey* (1963) 107 SJ 512, a clause which allowed for payment of a 'fixed salary . . . as a first charge on profits' was construed by the Court of Appeal as meaning a first payment out of the profit, and not a payment irrespective of whether or not there was sufficient profit to cover the payment.

It is usual to provide that the outgoings of the firm in respect of partners' expenses shall be treated as an expense of the firm (and not therefore as part of the partners' income). Further s 24(2) of the Partnership Act provides that the firm must indemnify each partner for payments made by them in the 'ordinary and proper conduct of the business of the firm'. These two provisions, linked together, will ensure that a partner is paid any expenses he incurs, but that such payment is not treated as a payment in respect of profit.

Losses are to be shared equally in the absence of an agreement (see s 24(1), p 78), but where it has been agreed that profits should be shared in a certain proportion, then it is implied that losses should be shared in the same proportion. However, for the avoidance of doubt it is usual to include a specific clause in the agreement either specifying that losses are to be borne in a particular ratio, or that they should be borne in the same ratio in which the partners are entitled to profits.

9 Negative and positive covenants

At this stage of the drafting of articles, it is necessary for the partners to decide what the other partners in the firm should not be permitted to do whilst still being partners and what they should be permitted to do. Thus it is usual to include a clause prohibiting partners from competing with the partnership business either indirectly or directly. If a partner is in breach of this clause, then by s 30 of the Partnership Act he must account for and pay over to the firm all profits made by this competing business. Although s 30 also prohibits a partner from carrying on business of the same nature as and competing with that of the firm without the consent of his co-partners, it is usual to provide expressly a covenant of this type so as to define specifically the areas which are prohibited. Further negative covenants in the articles might include restrictions on the partners' right to hire or fire employees (so that this could only be done by a majority of all partners) and prohibition of certain acts without the previous consent of the other partners (eg in the case of solicitors, giving security to any person).

It is also common to include a clause limiting the partners' authority in certain circumstances. It must be remembered that merely restricting the authority in the agreement will not, of itself, protect partners as against third parties. The latter are not bound by that restriction unless they know of the restriction or do not believe that they are dealing with a partner (see pp 11–13). Practically, the restriction should therefore limit a partner's power to draw upon the partnership bank account. This will at least give some protection against a partner's misappropriation, but will still not protect the partnership from contracts entered into with third parties without authority. There is very little that can be done in these circumstances apart from providing indemnities in the agreement and even such indemnities are not worth the paper they are written on in the event of the defaulting partner proving insolvent or where such a partner has disappeared (except in respect of his capital in the firm). The answer must ultimately lie in the relationship between the partners; if it is one of mutual trust and confidence, no restriction should be required; if it is not then the parties have no proper reason for entering into partnership.

A clause should provide that a partner should discharge his private debts promptly. Although his partners would not be liable for such debts, a private creditor could obtain judgment against an individual partner and enforce that judgment against the partner's partnership share by the appointment of a receiver or a charging order (s 23(2) of the Partnership Act). In the event of a charging order being made against an individual partner's share, the other partners are empowered by s 23(3) of the Partnership Act to redeem the interest so charged, or in the case of a sale being directed, to purchase that share. Since this could lead to the partnership being put in financial jeopardy, it is important to make a breach of this clause a possible ground for expulsion.

Positive covenants should also be included whereby all partners agree to devote their full time and attention to partnership affairs (or such time as the partners may agree) and also, as is the practice in most professionally drawn partnership articles, a clause spelling out the partners' duty of good faith to one another. This latter clause takes the form of a mutual covenant by each partner to be fair and true in all dealings with his fellow partners. This is of course always implied in any partnership (see p 22) but an express clause serves the purpose of reminding the partners of this important doctrine. (Also the expulsion clause can specify that breaches of these clauses can be a good reason for expelling a partner.)

10 Bankers

Whilst it may seem incongruous for the partners to have to be told who their bankers are in the partnership agreement, a clause which specifies the bankers is often included. It is also usual to specify in this clause who can sign the cheques. It may be that each partner can sign up to a specified amount and thereafter two partners are required to sign.

Of course, there is no requirement that only partners may sign cheques. Express authority for employees to sign cheques (eg the chief cashier) can be given if the partners see fit. However, if the partnership is one of solicitors, then with regard to the signing of client account cheques, r 11(7) of the Solicitors' Accounts Rules 1975 must be complied with. This provides:

> no money may be withdrawn from a bank account, being . . . a client account otherwise than under the signature of one at least of the following . . . namely (a) a solicitor who holds a current practising certificate, or (b) an employee of such a solicitor being either a solicitor or a Fellow of the Institute of Legal Executives . . . who shall have been admitted a Fellow for not less than five years.

Rule 3 of the 1975 Rules provides that all clients' money (as defined by the Rules) must without delay be paid into a client account. In a solicitors' firm the articles should specify this, so that all partners are reminded of this duty. Breaches of the account rules are the commonest cause of action being taken against solicitors before the Solicitors' Disciplinary Tribunal. The tribunal's predecessor (the Disciplinary Committee) held that where solicitors practising in partnership are in breach of the accounts rules, all partners are liable for the breach, not just the defaulting partners. The reason for this is the collective responsibility of the partners for the accounts. The penalty imposed on individual partners will, however, depend on all the circumstances including knowledge of the breach or whether a particular partner contributed to the breach through neglect. Consequently, the duty to comply with the Accounts Rules should be specified in the articles since whilst an innocent partner will nevertheless be liable for any breach, his penalty may be lighter if he shows that his defaulting co-partner was also in breach of the partnership articles.

It is unlikely that an express indemnity in the agreement would assist the innocent partners. First because the penalty exacted by either the Law Society's Professional Purposes Committee or the Disciplinary Tribunal may not amount to a financial one; secondly it is possible that such a clause would be void as being contrary to public policy.

11 Books of account, annual accounts and accountants

Whilst in most partnerships there is no legal reason to keep accounts, all partnerships will in practice keep detailed accounts of the financial affairs of the firm. The reasons for this are numerous and obvious. Each year the Revenue will require evidence of the profit the firm has made to enable an assessment of tax to be made. Other outsiders will also wish to see the accounts: for example the bank manager, if a substantial loan is required, or any potential partner who wishes to assess the financial viability of the firm. An annual account will also be taken so that each partner's entitlement to profits can be assessed. Consequently, the articles should specify that books of account should be kept, and the date in each year when an annual account should be made up. Further, it may be desirable to name the firm's accountants in the articles.

Sections 24(9) and 28 of the Partnership Act deal specifically with the accounts of the firm:

> **24(9).** The partnership books are to be kept at the place of business of the partnership (or the principal place, if there is more than one) and every partner may, when he thinks fit, have access to and inspect and copy any of them.
>
> **28.** Partners are bound to render true accounts and full information of all things affecting the partnership to any partner or his legal representative.

Subject to contrary agreement, s 24(9) provides not only for the place where the accounts are to be kept but also who can inspect and copy them. This latter point has been extended by case law to allow partners to instruct an agent to examine the accounts on their behalf. The case of *Bevan* v *Webb* [1901] 2 Ch 59 is authority for the following propositions:

1 Such an agent must be unobjectionable, ie be such a person to whom no reasonable objection could be taken.
2 No partner or agent can use the information so ascertained for an improper purpose.
3 The agent may be required to give an undertaking to this effect.

Section 28 has been dealt with before (see p 24) and because of the partners' overriding duty of good faith, this section cannot be excluded by express agreement.

In a solicitors' practice care must be taken to comply with the Solicitors' Accounts Rules 1975. This means that two bank accounts will have to be opened, the name of one account including the word 'client' (r 2(1)). All clients' money (as defined by r 2(1)) must be paid into such bank account without delay (r 3). This rule is subject to certain minor exceptions (see r 9). Since the solicitor can only withdraw money from his client bank account in specified circumstances (see r 7) care must be taken to instruct the bank that all payment of bank and interest charges to the bank should be made from the second bank account (usually called the office bank account, such account being the normal partnership bank account). Rule 11 specifies the type of accounts required to be kept, but is only concerned with those accounts which keep a record of dealings with clients' money. Such accounts much be preserved for at least six years from the last date of entry therein (r 11(6)).

Other professional partnerships are bound to keep accounts according to their own professional rules. For example, licensed stockbrokers must keep accounts in accordance with the Licensed Dealers (Conduct of Business) Rules 1960 (SI 1960 No 1216), and although at the time of writing s 4 of the Estate Agents Act 1979 has not been brought into force, this requires estate agents to maintain a separate client account subject to accounts regulations to be made by the Secretary of State for Prices and Consumer Protection.

The articles should also include a provision whereby after a specified time the accounts should not be reopened. If the accounts are drawn up in good faith, it is extremely useful to have such a clause to prevent a later re-allocation of profits. The clause can either state that after each partner has signed the accounts they are deemed conclusive, or it can provide that if any manifest error is discovered in them within six months of the partners' signature, it shall be rectified. However, if the latter type of clause is used, 'manifest error' only includes errors in figures arising from obvious mistakes, and not for example errors in judgment. These clauses will clearly not apply where a partner has been induced into signing the accounts by the fraud of his co-partner. In these circumstances the consequent breach of the defaulting partner's duty of good faith will mean that new accounts will be taken.

12 Retirement

Provision should be made for a situation arising where a partner is absent for long periods of time through sickness or ill health. In the absence of such an agreement, the other partners have two options open to them. If they can dissolve by notice, then they can give notice and set up again by themselves. This, however, will have serious tax consequences assuming that the sick partner is unwilling to join in an election under s 154 of the Income and Corporation Taxes Act 1970: the closing year rules will apply to the old partnership and the opening year rules will apply to the new one (see p 35). Further, it may take the other partners up to one year to give notice of their retirement in the event of a clause providing for expiry of notice on the date of the annual account. During this time the sick partner is entitled to his share of the profit and the remaining partners are unable to pay themselves extra for the additional workload imposed by the absence of one of their partners. Whilst the case of *Airey* v *Borham* (1861) 29 Beav 620 is authority for the fact that the court can, in certain circumstances, order a partner to pay compensation where he is guilty of not attending to his work, this will only apply where there is a wilful failure to assist in the business, not where a partner, through no fault of his own, is unable to work.

The alternative for the other partners, faced with an unhealthy partner, and without express provision in the agreement, is to apply to the court under s 35 of the Partnership Act for the court to dissolve the partnership on the grounds that the partner suffering from ill health is permanently incapable of performing his part of the partnership contract. Even this is not the best of answers; as with most applications to the court in partnership matters, this is an application made to the Chancery Division of the High Court. It may mean several months elapse before the application is heard, and again the partnership must continue to pay the absent partner. Problems may also arise over the interpretation of the word 'permanently' in s 35. An illness of one year's duration does not necessarily mean a partner is permanently incapable of continuing.

Under s 103(1)(*f*) of the Mental Health Act 1959, a judge can order dissolution of a partnership by reason of a partner suffering mental illness. (The Partnership Act does not apply in this case.) Mental disorder does not of itself dissolve a partnership (see *Waters* v *Taylor* (1813) 2 Yes & B 299), and it is therefore wise for the remaining partners to seek an interlocutory injunction to prevent the mentally ill partner from interfering with the management of the business. Before a judge will order dissolution he must be satisfied that there is mental disorder (*Sadler* v *Lee* (1843) 6 Beav 324), but once ordered, the costs of dissolution can be paid from the partnership assets (*Jones* v *Welch* (1855) 1 K & J 765). The judge in ordering a dissolution is seeking not only to protect the remaining partners but also the mentally ill partner. He has assets within the firm that he is no longer capable of protecting, thus the Court of Protection takes over the control and protection of these assets.

To avoid these clumsy applications and doubt over when such applications can be made, provision should be made in the deed for compulsory retirement after, say, 100 days absence. Partners will have to decide whether such 100 days should be consecutive before they can exercise the right, or whether any 100 days in a calendar year will suffice. Equally if a partner allows his fellow partner time off over the limit imposed by the agreement, to safeguard his own interests he should give the incapable partner notice that such allowance does not amount to a waiver of his rights under the agreement.

In order to safeguard a partner's own position in the event of his suffering serious illness, he should consider the possibility of taking out sickness and disability insurance. Not only will this give him an income in the event of illness, but it will also help the other partners to come to a commercial decision when considering invoking any compulsory retirement provision. Whilst premiums for such insurance are not deductible for tax purposes, the schemes are so attractive that consideration should be given to making them compulsory by imposing a condition in the partnership agreement.

The longer a partner pays into a retirement scheme, the better the benefits available when he reaches retirement age. A partner who has worked for forty years in a partnership is entitled to expect recompense when he retires. During this period he will have built up his capital in the firm, and will therefore have a lump sum to look forward to on retirement. This, as has been seen, could lead to some financial embarrassment on the part of his younger partners, especially if the sum is a large one. The partnership agreement should therefore provide that whilst a lump sum is paid to the retiring partner, this should be just the first instalment, and the balance should be paid with interest over such number of years as is equitable from all parties' points of view, bearing in mind the sum involved. In the absence of such an agreement s 42 of the Partnership Act would apply (see p 78). Some thought should also be given to the repayment of capital before retirement. If a partner is to retire at sixty-five, there is no reason why, providing the firm has the cash, he should not be paid part of his capital by instalments over the five years prior to retirement. Care should be taken to ensure that a senior partner does not increase his capital contributions during the years leading up to retirement because this, of course, will just increase the problem.

One further option open to the partners who must ultimately provide for the repayment of capital is to take advantage of partnership life assurance where a lump sum becomes payable on death or when a partner achieves a stated age. This will, if used properly, provide the cash available to repay capital, thus benefiting the firm by reducing or discharging its liability to the outgoing partner; and the outgoing partner is also happy since he gets an immediate cash payment without waiting for the bulk to be paid by instalments over a number of years. A number of schemes are available, and a scheme should be chosen which not only gives income tax relief on payment of the premium, but also avoids capital taxes either during the period insured or at the end of such period.

Capital is not the only valuable commodity a partner owns in the firm. His other saleable item is the goodwill he has built up over the years he has been associated with the firm. Indeed, when he joined the firm as a partner some thirty or forty years ago, he may well have paid for goodwill by putting some money into the firm by way of a premium (or making a payment outside the accounts to the other partners) as the purchase price for his share of the goodwill. The modern trend in most professional partnerships is for incoming partners not to pay for goodwill. A decision as to how goodwill is to be dealt with must be taken by a new partnership as soon as possible. If incoming partners are not to pay for it, outgoing partners equally cannot expect to be paid for it, despite its unquestionable value. If this decision is made, then certain action must be taken.

First, as has already been mentioned (see p 54) goodwill is an asset of the firm accruing to each partner equally in the absence of an agreement. Therefore on retirement a partner is entitled to take his share of goodwill with him, or alternatively he will negotiate with his co-partners for the sale to them of this asset. Equally on a partner's death this asset will devolve upon his personal representatives, and it will be up to the remaining partners to negotiate with them. It is therefore necessary for the partners expressly to provide that on the retirement or death of a partner his share in any goodwill shall not be valued, but shall accrue automatically to the remaining partners, in the share in which they share profits without payment by them. Ideally this agreement should be embodied in the terms of the partnership articles. Such a clause may lead to capital tax implications, but in most cases it should be possible to avoid the payment of any tax. The goodwill accrual could amount to a disposition for capital gains tax purposes by the retiring partner to the remaining partners. However, applying the Inland Revenue Statement of Practice of 17 January 1975 (see Appendix 2) providing there is no revaluation of the goodwill, or no payment 'outside the accounts', and provided that it is a *bona fide* commercial transaction, no tax will be payable. As to capital transfer tax, the absence of cash consideration may pose a problem, but one which is easily surmounted providing some consideration can be found. It is assumed that the old estate duty cases of *Att-Gen* v *Boden* [1912] 1 KB 539 and *Att-Gen* v *Ralli* (1936) 15 ATC 523 are still effective for this purpose. These cases held that sufficient consideration is to be found in the commercial nature of the transactions, and the mutual covenants and obligations of the partners. If despite the partners' precautions (or maybe because of them) tax is payable then some relief should be available for capital gains tax in the form of hold over relief (s 79 of the Finance Act 1980) or 'retirement relief' under s 124 of the Capital Gains Tax Act 1979 (see p 43); further the 'business property' relief (Finance Act 1976, s 73 as amended) will possibly exempt any payment of capital transfer tax (see p 48).

The second point to arise from the partners' decision to let goodwill automatically accrue to the remaining partners, is that the retiring partner will need to be compensated for the loss of this valuable asset. If he is not to receive any cash payment for it he will need some alternative means to see him through his retirement. One common way of achieving this goal is to provide in the partnership articles that each partner, on attaining a specified age, shall become a member of a retirement benefit scheme. The money paid by the partners under these schemes will provide a retirement annuity for their retirement, the main advantage of such a scheme being that it can give valuable tax advantages to the paying partners. So important is this advantage that consideration should be given to making such schemes compulsory by a provision in the partnership deed requiring that premiums paid by each partner should be of the maximum amounts.

To qualify for tax relief, the payment must be made to a scheme which is approved by the Inland Revenue under the Income and Corporation Taxes Act 1970, s 226. To obtain approval the main object of the scheme must be to provide the individual partner with a life annuity in old age, or an annuity for the spouse or dependants of a deceased partner. The maximum amount which can be paid into such a scheme is limited to 'qualifying premiums', Qualifying premiums are 17½% of net relevant earnings (Finance Act 1980). Provision is made for a higher relief for older contributors by the Finance Act 1982. Such premiums are allowable in full as a deduction from a partner's relevant earnings. Net relevant earnings are defined in s 227 of the Income and Corporation Taxes Act (as amended by the Finance Act 1980) as a partner's share of the partnership earnings on the preceding year basis less charges which are directly related to the business in question. This will therefore include capital allowances and losses, other business expenses, and also an annuity to a former partner paid by the firm (as to such annuities see p 156). A further provision of the Finance Act 1980 allows unclaimed relief to be carried forward and used in any of the following six years of assessment. This means that in those subsequent years, if there is unclaimed relief from previous year(s) the limit of 17½% of net relevant earnings can be exceeded to the extent of the unclaimed relief, and such premiums paid are fully deductible. So far as the recipient of the annuity is concerned it is treated as earned income in his hands to the extent that the premiums were allowed for tax purposes. Any other income from the scheme will be treated as investment income and thus may attract the investment income surcharge.

In addition to a scheme providing an annuity or pension for their retirement, the partners may also wish to avail themselves of an insurance policy which provides an annuity for the spouse or dependants of the partner (or indeed a lump sum payment) on the death of the partner before a specified date being before he attained the age of seventy-five. This scheme also has tax advantages provided it falls within s 226A of the Income and Corporation Taxes Act 1970. The premiums paid will be fully deductible from a partner's relevant earnings. There is, however, a maximum sum which can be paid to qualify for tax relief, and this sum is currently (Finance Act 1980) 5% of net relevant earnings.

It should be appreciated that when planning for retirement a partner can pay up to 17½% of his net relevant earnings in schemes to provide for annuities under s 226 and s 226A. However, of that 17½% only 5% of net relevant earnings can be spent on a s 226A policy. If therefore a partner's net relevant earnings amounted to £20,000 then 17½% of this figure (£3,500) may be paid as a qualifying premium. Of this up to £1,000 (ie 5%) may be spent on s 226A policies.

These schemes will not assist the more senior partners whose firm decide no longer to make payments for goodwill in the future. It is no good providing an agreement requiring a fifty-year-old partner to contribute to a retirement annuity scheme as outlined above because the premiums will be too high; he will have to look for other or additional means of being compensated for the loss of payment for his goodwill. These alternative means include the firm itself paying the retired partner an annuity out of future profits of the business. This annuity may still be relevant even if there is no requirement for a partner to be compensated for loss of goodwill: there may be clear commercial reasons to pay it. To gain a tax advantage from this scheme, certain important conditions must be satisfied (see p 157). This scheme does have one major disadvantage compared to pensions paid under s 226 of the Income and Corporation Taxes Act 1970, in that the retired partner must rely upon the continued success of the business of the partnership for payment to be made to him. If there is a fall in profits this must mean a fall in the retired partner's annuity. Equally, from the point of the continuing partners, this scheme is a burden upon their future profits despite the favourable tax concessions. If possible, it is better from all points of view to provide in the articles for partners to contribute towards their own pensions using the advantages of s 226 policies.

One further problem that can arise on the firm paying annuities to a retired partner is the possibility of capital gains tax liability. This is discussed in detail on pp 156–158.

As far as solicitors are concerned, for the partners to provide for an annuity out of profits, they must take advantage of the general waiver granted by the Law Society of r 3 of the Solicitors' Practice Rules 1936–72. Rule 3 provides that a solicitor shall not share or agree to share his professional fees with any person except (among others) another solicitor. A retired partner whilst remaining on the Roll will not necessarily go to the expense of renewing his practising certificate and will not therefore be entitled to share profits of his former firm. However, the Law Society has given a general waiver dated 28 July 1972 in the following terms:

> A solicitor in practice may pay or agree to pay an annuity or other sum out of professional fees to a retired partner or predecessor or the dependants or personal representatives of a deceased partner or predecessor.

Finally, the partners may wish to provide for their retirement by coming to an arrangement whereby the retired partner is offered a consultancy agreement with the firm. This will clearly have tax advantages to both sides in that any sum payable by the firm is deductible provided it is paid wholly and exclusively for the purposes of the partnership. If a consultant is paid an inflated fee, then the excess will not be deductible as an expense (see *Copeman* v *Flood* [1941] 1 KB 202). In the hands of the consultant the payment should be taxed as earned income under Schedule D, Case II; that is he should be treated as an independent contractor and not an employee. If this is so then not only will he be taxed on the preceding year basis (for the advantages of which see p 35), but he will also be able to claim deductions for expenses incurred. If a consultant solicitor requires his name to be on the headed notepaper of the firm, he must comply with the Solicitors' Practice Rules 1967 which permit only the name of a solicitor holding a current practising certificate to be printed on the professional notepaper of the firm. Since invariably a consultant will require his name on the notepaper this will mean additional expense. This is a further argument in favour of a Schedule D, Case II assessment, for the practising certificate fee and compensation fund contribution will be deductible. In addition to the consultant's name on the notepaper there should be some indication of his status. If his name is merely added to those of the other partners then he could be said to be holding himself out as a partner, and under s 14 of the Partnership Act incur liability as a partner for certain partnership debts (see p 19).

It is usual as part of the entire package providing for death or retirement of a partner to include a clause restraining the retired partner from competing with the partnership, usually for a specified period of time within a specified area. Where there has been a sale of goodwill the law protects the buyer's interest even if no specific agreement is reached, in that the seller of goodwill will be restrained from soliciting the customers of the firm. Thus, where one partner leaves the firm, and either sells his share of the goodwill to the other partners, or where the partnership agreement provides for an automatic accrual of goodwill to the remaining partners, then even in the absence of a covenant in restraint of trade, the remaining partners will be able to restrain the retired partner from canvassing the customers of the firm. This, however, is in itself insufficient protection for the continuing partners as there is no reason why the retired partner should not deal with the firm's customers or clients if they come to him of their own accord. Therefore a specific restrictive covenant is usually imposed on retirement, such covenant appearing in the partnership deed.

To be enforceable, a covenant which restrains a retired partner from engaging in businesses within a radius of, eg, five miles from the firm's principal place of business for a period of two years must satisfy certain conditions. The historical position was that such covenants in restraint of trade were void as being contrary to public policy (see, eg, *Rogers* v *Parrey* (1613) 2 Bulst 136). However, the modern trend is to permit such covenants provided that they are 'reasonable'. Each case will be looked at on its own merits, and what is reasonable in one set of circumstances may not be in another. Much will depend on the catchment area served by the firm, and clearly any attempt in a covenant to extend the restriction beyond this area will be unreasonable and therefore void. Additionally the clause should not be contrary to the public interest. It is possible to envisage a situation where a clause might satisfy the test of reasonableness but might be contrary to the public interest; eg a small firm of solicitors practising in a country area with little or no competition from other firms over a relatively large catchment area. In such a case, were one partner to leave it might be reasonable to restrict him from setting up within the catchment area for a specified time, but it might also be contrary to public interest that the original firm should retain the monopoly of legal services in that area.

13 Income tax election

In order that the remaining partners can elect for the firm to be treated as continuing in respect of payment of income tax (see p 142) there should be an obligation imposed upon the retiring partner (or his personal representatives) to join with the remaining partners in making the necessary election under s 154(2) of the Income and Corporation Taxes Act 1970 (see p 142). The retiring partner will, however, in such circumstances want an indemnity from the remaining partners so that if he suffers any extra tax as a result of the election, he may be indemnified by the remaining partners.

14 Expulsion

As well as providing for voluntary retirement by partners, it is prudent to include in the articles provisions relating to compulsory retirement. Section 25 of the Partnership Act provides that 'No majority of the partners can expel any partner unless a power to do so has been conferred by express agreement between the partners.' Thus it is vital to include a provision before any circumstances arise which might give rise to partners wishing to exercise such a right.

The expulsion clause should be drafted so that breaches of specific clauses in the deed can lead to expulsion, eg the clause requiring a partner to devote the whole of his time to the business, the clause emphasising the duty of good faith, a clause requiring punctual payment of private debts, and any of the negative covenants in the deed, eg the agreement not to carry on a competing or any other business without consent. The clause can be drafted to include other specific occasions when a partner may be expelled, eg for failure to account for moneys within a certain time, if he becomes bankrupt, if he turns to 'betting, gambling or notorious intemporance or immorality or other scandalous conduct'.

A firm that expels a partner must do so for the benefit of the firm and not for the personal gain of the remaining partners. To expel a partner in the latter case is in breach of the duty of good faith and the expulsion can be set aside by the court. In *Blisset* v *Daniel* (1853) 10 Hare 493 a partner was expelled and his share purchased at a low valuation as provided for in the deed; his presence within the firm had not been detrimental to it, he had been expelled because the other partners wanted a greater share of the property and profits. The court set aside the expulsion.

It is also usual to provide in the clause how it is to be notified to the offending partner, eg in writing with immediate effect. This latter point is very important because if a partner is doing serious damage to the firm it is imperative that he be removed as quickly as possible. Even if it were a partnership at will without an expulsion clause, the only way of effecting the equivalent of an expulsion would be to dissolve the firm completely which would give the offending partner rights to force a sale of the assets and give him continuing authority in the winding up of the firm. If he is expelled with immediate effect and the articles provide that the expulsion will dissolve the firm only in so far as he is concerned, then the remaining partners are not at risk (nor can any other partner seize the opportunity to leave the firm). In addition, the clause should specify that the remaining partners have the right to notify their clients and customers of the fact that a partner has departed from the firm.

So that the expelled partner cannot demand his share of the partnership assets immediately which would otherwise be his right, the articles should provide how he is to be paid his share. The same terms as apply on retirement can be made to apply to expulsion, although the clause might provide for payment to be made, eg, over a longer period

15 Death

Section 33(1) of the Partnership Act provides 'subject to any agreement between the partners, every partnership is dissolved as regards all partners by the death . . . of any partner'. Whilst this clause will not be of concern to a two partner firm, care should be taken when further partners are introduced. Obviously on the death of one of two partners, the firm is dissolved, and the remaining individual, if he carries on business, will do so as a sole trader or practitioner. When there are three or more partners it is clearly inconvenient for the whole firm to be dissolved by the death of one of them (as to the consequences of dissolution see p 52). The agreement should therefore state clearly that the death of one partner will not dissolve the partnership as regards the remaining partners. The financial consequences of such death should also be clearly stated, and it is usual to link these in with the retirement provisions, allowing the continuing partners to pay off capital by instalments, or pay annuities to the personal representatives of the deceased or his dependants or spouse.

16 Dissolution

The articles may, if desired, give further grounds for dissolution of the firm. In the absence of such grounds, and in the absence of a specific duration clause, the Partnership Act will apply. The articles may also vary the way in which the assets and liabilities are to be dealt with on a complete dissolution of the firm (rather than, eg, on retirement of one partner), eg by excluding goodwill from the assets to be realised under s 39 of the Partnership Act (see p 52).

17 Documents

Particularly in a partnership of solicitors there should be provision in the articles relating to deeds and documents which belong to the firm and also those which belong to clients. It should be made clear that on retirement all such documents should be handed over to the remaining partners. This agreement will not prejudice any client of the firm who wishes the retiring partner to continue to act for him. In that case, however, the remaining partners (ie the firm) have a lien over the client's papers for unpaid costs. However, it seems that in certain cases for all practical purposes this lien will be lost since the firm can be compelled to hand over those papers 'subject to lien' (see *Cordery on Solicitors*, 7th ed, Butterworths, 1981).

18 Arbitration

Certainly in most professional partnerships it is usual to provide for an arbitration clause whereby disputes between partners involving the firm's affairs are settled privately by an arbitrator as opposed to publicly in open court. The relevant legislation is to be found in the Arbitration Acts 1950–79 which allow the court (in any application to which the arbitration clause might apply) to stay the proceedings in order that the matter may be referred to the arbitrator in accordance with the clause. This ensures that the partners use the provisions as to arbitration in the articles rather than risk the adverse publicity which might arise from any dispute being aired in open court. The clause, if it allows arbitration on all matters relating to the partnership, will also be effective in relation to any claim for dissolution, and in this case the arbitrator has the power to dissolve the partnership (see *Vawdrey* v *Simpson* [1896] 1 Ch 166). If the partners wish the clause to be binding on those persons claiming through a partner (eg an assignee of a share in the partnership) the clause must specifically provide for this. The clause must not be so widely drawn that it ousts the jurisdiction of the courts completely, or the courts will not have regard to it. It is usual in a solicitors' deed of partnership to provide that the arbitrator shall be nominated by the President of the Law Society for the time being.

Chapter 8

Day to Day Business

1 Management

It is probably a truism to say that a successful firm is a well run firm. Whether solicitors make good managers is questionable; as the Preface to *Organisation and Management of a Solicitor's Practice* (looseleaf, Oyez Longman) says: 'Solicitors in general are notoriously bad managers.' Although management is not really a question of law, more of good sense and efficiency, it may be sensible to start with a look at whatever assistance the law may give. The relevant parts of s 24 of the Act lay down a code of practice for the running of a partnership, part or all of which can be changed by contrary agreement.

'Every partner may take part in the management of the business' (s 24(4)). Indeed, every partner is impliedly or expressly bound to take part in the running of the business. Exactly what part he may take in the management of the firm will depend on the nature and size of the firm. In many of the bigger firms a different task of management (eg office and library administration) is allotted to each partner and indeed such a partner may be entitled by the terms of the partnership agreement to a salary for performing this management function. If a partner is excluded from the management of the firm, unless he has previously agreed to being so excluded, this will be grounds for asking the court to dissolve the firm under s 35. The articles will very often, however, express a contrary intention—junior partners may be excluded from being involved in certain decisions, a dormant partner might be excluded from management decisions altogether.

'No partner may be introduced as a partner without the consent of all existing partners' (s 24(7)). This subsection can, like the others, be overridden by contrary agreement but it is probably advisable, anyway in a small firm, to ensure that the decision needs unanimous consent. In a larger firm it is obviously impracticable for the prospective partner to be interviewed by all fifty or so partners but on the other hand the final decision, on the recommendation of a few partners, should be taken by as many partners as possible.

'Any difference arising as to ordinary matters connected with the partnership business may be decided by a majority of the partners, but no change may be made in the nature of the partnership business without the consent of all existing partners' (s 24(8)). The Act thus envisages that changes in the membership of the firm and the nature of the business should generally be with the consent of all the partners although this can be overridden by contrary agreement. In a solicitors' firm the latter point does not raise many problems as it is not possible within the rules of the profession to decide, eg, to diversify and run an estate agent's business. What exactly amounts to an 'ordinary matter' is not exactly clear and there is very little case law on the topic. It probably includes decisions on capital expenditure, location of office premises, and employees, but inevitably what is an ordinary matter in one partnership may not be so in another particularly in view of the size of the firm. By the partnership articles matters over and above those dealt with in the Act may be required to have unanimous consent, eg an increase in capital contributions, or the place of business (see *Clements* v *Norris* (1878) 8 Ch D 129). Although the decision may be arrived at by the majority unless otherwise agreed, it is part of the duty of good faith of partners that the majority should consult with the minority on any such issues. If there is no such consultation then the aggrieved partners could seek to have the decision set aside (see *Const* v *Harris* (1824) T & R 496). As well as consulting the other partners, the majority must act for the benefit of the whole firm and not just their own interests, otherwise the duty of good faith has again been broken. If the voting partners are split equally on a decision, the Act gives no help, but it has been decided that those who support the existing situation will triumph; there will be no change (*Donaldson* v *Williams* (1833) 1 Cr & M 345). Some provision should therefore be made or considered as to whether there should be a partner with a casting vote.

What should therefore be decided (and possibly incorporated in the articles) about the management of the firm?

First, any limitation on the authority of a partner in the general business and management of the firm should be considered, eg whether all partners have the right to sign cheques or whether all partners have the right to enter into contracts of any value.

Secondly, the duties of management can be emphasised. It is usual to find in a partnership deed a clause emphasising the duty of all partners to take part in the management and business of the firm. Failure to carry out this duty may be a ground for dissolution of the firm or expulsion of the offending partner. The clause usually requires a partner to devote 'the whole of his time' to the business which on the face of it gives him no right to a holiday of any kind. Thus the clause usually continues with the holiday entitlement of the partners. Some partnership deeds today not only state the number of weeks holiday to which a partner is entitled but also state that that partner is bound to take that amount of holiday. This is obviously intended to preserve him for the continuing benefit of the firm.

Thirdly, the responsibilities of each partner can be decided. It is first necessary to identify the various areas of responsibility. To give a general indication these are some of the matters to be considered.

Finance: this includes book-keeping and accounts department, compliance with the Solicitors' Accounts Rules 1975; any system of time recording; monitoring financial performance; and budgeting.

Premises: leases and renewals of leases; repairs and the general state and condition of the premises.

Staff: not only the hiring and firing of staff but also staff relations which are essential to the smooth running of the office.

Office equipment: making sure that business machinery from the simplest typewriter to the most sophisticated computer is being used to best effect; replacing these when necessary; and deciding whether it is better to lease or to buy.

Books and conferences: an adequate and up to date library is essential but expensive and it is important to make best use of the finance available—this can only be done with planning.

Future planning: the future development of the firm must be actively considered bearing in mind the experience of the members of the firm, outside economic factors and the like.

General management: there are countless day to day matters that also have to be considered, eg all the various types of insurance from professional indemnity insurance to insuring the contents of the office, and office stationery.

In a firm run by a sole practitioner the overall responsibility for all of these matters is borne by one person; the larger the firm is the more is it possible and indeed necessary to divide up these responsibilities. In many of the large firms there is a partner who never does any legal work in relation to clients at all; he is, as management partner, fully concerned with the running of the office. One further point for consideration is that many of the tasks can be delegated with a specified partner having overall responsibility only. In this way the time of a major fee earner is not taken up with the minutiae of his area of responsibility and can be put to better use earning fees.

Many of these areas of responsibility necessitate the taking of decisions and these decisions and any others must be taken in the proper way. Some decisions will require the unanimous consent of all the partners; other decisions can be taken by a majority of partners; some decision-making powers particularly on the day to day administration of the firm can be left to an individual partner who carries that responsibility. It is sensible to hold regular partners' meetings and to decide how often these are to be held. Meetings should be held at least once a month and may be needed more often; a possibility could be that a number of the more senior partners meet once a week to discuss and if necessary make certain decisions and all the partners meet at least once a month. In some of the bigger firms it is just not feasible to have many meetings with all the partners and many of the decisions are taken by partners' committees who then merely report to the others on what has been decided.

The Young Solicitors' Group of the Law Society has published a booklet entitled *A Guide to Partnership Problems and Pitfalls* which is intended for those about to embark on being a partner. It stresses that: 'These days, a partner must be a shrewd businessman, a capable administrator and an understanding personnel manager as well as being a good solicitor.'

2 Day to day finance

There are two types of capital—fixed capital and working capital. Fixed capital is that which is required for the permanent assets of the firm—the premises, furniture, machinery (typewriters, photocopiers, etc) books. The money for this can be provided by the partners themselves or it can be found by some sort of long-term borrowing from the bank or from one of the insurance companies. If the money is provided by the partners then, as we have already seen, this must be recorded in their capital accounts and will be repayable to them when they leave the firm. The more capital a partner has in the firm the more problems may be created on his retirement; the remaining partners may have no way of realising the assets, eg the office premises, to pay the retiring partner. The only way they may be able to pay him is to get his agreement to be paid in instalments or by way of an annuity (see p 153), to borrow, or to take on a new partner who will be expected to bring in capital or repay the retiring partner. This of course only perpetuates the problem. The other way of funding the capital needed for fixed assets is to borrow. The main drawbacks to borrowing are that the present high interest rates mean that not only must the capital repayments but so also must the heavy interest repayments be found out of the firm's income. In addition the lender is likely to require some security—either personal guarantees or a mortgage over the office premises.

The other type of capital is what is known as working capital (sometimes referred to as net current assets); that is what is necessary to finance the day to day expenses of running the firm—the wages and salaries of the employees, the rent and repair bill, the twice-yearly tax bill, insurance and the like. Although these items are usually paid from income, working capital is needed because there is not always a sufficient amount of income at any one time to meet these outgoings. Work in progress has got to be funded, bills for work already done may not yet have been sent out or clients may take a long time to pay their bills. In addition, there are at different times of the year major items of expenditure which have to be funded by income earned throughout the year, eg the tax bill. Working capital can be funded by short-term borrowing from the bank; or the partners themselves can fund the working capital requirements by leaving a proportion of profits in the firm, ie not drawing out all the profit to which they are entitled. The latter method has drawbacks—first, all undrawn profit is credited to the partner's current account which may increase the problem of what happens on his retirement; secondly, the younger partners particularly may not be able to afford to leave in undrawn profits as they are likely to be at a time of high expenditure in their lives and to be receiving a smaller share of the profits than the senior partners.

A solution to the specific problem of the tax bill may be to create what is known as a tax reserve so that when the time comes, the tax does not have to be paid either by the partners out of their own pockets or by borrowing from the bank. This tax reserve can be created by keeping back from each partner an amount of profit sufficient to meet his share of the tax bill. This has the additional benefit of increasing working capital. How exactly the right amount of the reserve is calculated is open to argument. The methods range from a maximum reserve, ie reserving for all future taxes payable by reference to profits so far earned, to a minimum reserve, ie an amount to cover any instalment due, and the proportion of the next tax assessment which has accrued so far. In any event in calculating each partner's contribution to the reserve it is usual to give full credit for the personal and other allowances and deductions that will in practice be granted against his share of the firm's assessment.

The general problem in many firms is that they are over capitalised. Too much money is tied up in fixed assets and/or too much has been paid in by the partners either to purchase fixed assets or to fund working capital. Ideally the amount of capital in the firm should be at the level of about 90% of the profits.

There are ways of reducing capital. First, the level of fixed capital may not need to be so high. Is it necessary to own premises or would it be better to lease them? Remember that in a solicitors' firm rather than a trading firm, it is unlikely to be the aim of the partners to build up a large amount of capital and goodwill and then sell the business as a going concern for large profit. It may be possible therefore to sell the premises and lease them back; this will have the advantage of providing funds with which to pay back some of the partners' capital so that the problems on death or retirement are not so great. Is it necessary to buy office machinery? It is usually possible to lease machinery and provided a check is kept on whether the rent and repair bill is reasonable this may be the best way of providing for up to date office equipment, especially, eg, when new and better computers are being produced all the time. If goodwill is regarded as a capital asset of the firm, then consideration should be given to writing it out of the accounts (see p 89).

Working capital requirements can be reduced by improving cash flow. Sending out bills regularly and promptly results in less working capital being tied up in work in progress. In both contentious and non-contentious business the Solicitors Act 1974 allows interim bills to be sent out, thus in long drawn out litigation, or a lengthy probate matter, interim billing should be considered. Ascertain whether sufficient sums are being asked for on account of disbursements. Are bills being sent out promptly? If not, the firm is lengthening the time when it must depend on working capital rather than income. It must be remembered that billing has the effect of converting work in progress into debtors. Secondly, are clients paying quickly enough? While solicitors should obviously not indulge in strong arm tactics in recovering sums owed by clients, there is no need to wait for six months before gently reminding the client that he or she owes money. Thirdly, can the tax bill be reduced in any way as this provides probably the greatest distortion in cash flow? Has the best advantage been taken of capital allowances? The purchase of equipment or machinery for the office gives rise to a claim for capital allowances—up to 100% in the first year if it is so wished. At the end of a good accounting period, the firm could consider re-equipping then, rather than at another time. The maximum tax advantage could therefore be obtained. Of course, it has to be borne in mind that the capital cost of this equipment will have to be found.

The basis of taxation is important. In the first three years of the firm there is no choice and the earnings basis of accounting must be used, ie the tax bill will be calculated on the amount earned by the firm rather than the amount actually paid to the firm—thus tax is being paid on work in progress and unpaid bills. The other bases—the conventional bases—are, first, bills delivered when work in progress no longer comes into the calculation but unpaid bills do; secondly, the cash basis where tax is calculated only on the amounts actually received by the firm. The latter is obviously the best from the cash flow point of view although not inevitably the best as, eg, the earnings basis allows a claim for work in progress relief that may be advantageous. After three years in existence the firm should therefore consider whether it is sensible to change to a different basis of accounting. It will be desirable to consult the accountant and it is necessary to persuade the Revenue to allow the change. These matters are considered in more detail on pp 116–118.

The tax bill of the partners can also be reduced if they take the maximum advantage of the tax allowances for deductible expenditure. Certain personal expenses incurred on behalf of the firm can be deductible, eg car leasing or purchasing costs, salaries to wives or husbands, subscriptions and cost of periodicals, certain travelling, etc.

From this very brief discussion on day to day finance it can be seen that solicitors, and any other businessmen, must be very aware of the financial structure of the firm. They must be constantly alert to ways of improving cash flow, reducing borrowing and avoiding capital and countless other financial problems. They should budget for or plan their fees and expenses in this year and the year ahead; in a larger firm they should have a good system of reporting so that they know exactly what is going on and they should be prepared to look regularly at the financial situation so that immediate action can be taken to remedy any problem that occurs (as to ways of doing this see p 112).

3 Office efficiency

The Royal Commission on Legal Services recommended that 'all solicitors should review their practices and office procedures to ensure that they take full advantage of the efficiency and economy which can be obtained with the assistance of modern technology'. Many firms seem resistant to modern technology, preferring instead the time-honoured and time-costly methods that they have used for so long. The advantages of some form of time-costing system (rather than feeling the weight of the file) are discussed at pp 113–116. Other systems which may be useful are considered in (*a*)–(*c*) below.

(*a*) *Mechanised accounting systems*

These considerably reduce the man hours involved in a manual system, although the manual system may work well and change for change's sake should be avoided. In addition, these systems are able to provide the up to date information which is so necessary, and also produce details of the profitability of departments or even individuals, lists of debtors and various other data automatically. There is a choice between having your own mini-computer where everything is dealt with in the office, or taking advantage of one of the computer bureaux facilities available (see p 107).

(*b*) *Word processing equipment*

Typing repetitive documents takes time and therefore increases secretarial costs. Many leases for example contain the same clauses to a large extent. By the use of a word processor, standard type can be stored and retrieved where necessary. It will then be produced automatically without having to be typed all over again and is very easy to alter to suit the individual client. Where both word processors and accounting systems are concerned it should be remembered that one of the highest outgoings of a solicitors' firm is in staff costs and these machines can help to reduce these. Of course, the cost of buying or leasing them, and their running costs and whether this is justified bearing in mind the size and type of work of the firm, must be considered in depth.

(*c*) *Other computerised systems*

Firms which have large debt collecting departments, can increase profitability by installing a computerised system of debt collecting. What is known as information retrieval can be assisted by computer, eg finding precedents, names, addresses, files, etc. Finally, even the very basis of a solicitor's knowledge can be assisted by computer in that various systems are being developed which will store and provide immediate recall of the law. Instead of hours searching through the library (which is of course very up to date as the partner responsible is very efficient), the up to date statutory provision or regulation will be available at the touch of a button.

4 Accounts

The main purpose of keeping accounts is to keep an accurate record of the firm's financial affairs. In addition to this need, a further requirement is that an accurate record of all dealings with clients' money must be kept where the profession is that of a solicitor (see Solicitors' Accounts Rules 1975). An individual's choice of accounting system will clearly depend upon the particular circumstances involved. In the early years of a partnership the partners should be able to keep their own accounts and should ensure that these are written up every day to retain accuracy. However, as the office grows, so should the accounting system, which should eventually be put under the control of a suitably qualified cashier.

Systems are now available which use the latest technology and these mean that at any time the latest balance on any particular client's ledger account can be revealed. The more sophisticated systems involve either the firm having a video display unit and printer in the principal office, connected to an outside computer, or the installation of a small computer in the office itself. In either case the cashier can enter the data on a day to day (or hour to hour) basis and the accounts are immediately updated. There is access either by reference to the video display unit or, in a more permanent form, by the printer. The advantage of a small computer (which can be linked with a word processor) is the additional information that can be obtained. In addition to a full accounting system the computer can indicate the level of work in progress, and the level of debtors at regular intervals which can of course be of immense help to the busy practitioner. A time-costing scheme (see p 113) can be implemented through the use of such a system, and even future profit forecasts made. Most systems for use in a solicitors' office will have the Solicitors' Accounts Rules 1975 as part of their program so that any attempted breach of these rules will be immediately spotted by the computer and the cashier automatically informed.

Whatever system is used, at yearly intervals it will be necessary to consolidate the accounts into final accounts. These final accounts consist of (in a professional partnership) the profit and loss account, an appropriation account, and the balance sheet. Whilst this is not the place for a detailed study of accounts, and the interpretation of such accounts, partners should, of course, be sufficiently aware of the basic principles of accounting to understand their accounts, and the trends indicated by them.

The profit and loss account is the account where the gross fees of a partnership are stated (plus a sum in respect of work in progress, ie unbilled work). The expenses of the practice are set against this figure to reveal a net profit. This profit is then allocated to the partners in the appropriation section of the account in accordance with their profit-sharing ratio.

Example:
A and *B* are in partnership. They share profits as follows:
A receives a salary of £4,500
B receives a salary of £6,000. Thereafter profits are shared equally.

Profit and Loss Account
Year ending 31 December 198–

	£	£
Income		
Gross fees	80,000	
Work in progress	20,000	100,000
Less expenses		
Salaries to employees	10,000	
General expenses	57,000	
Insurances, etc	2,500	69,500
NET PROFIT		30,500

Appropriations		
Salary *A*	4,500	
Salary *B*	6,000	10,500
Balance divisible		
A (½)	10,000	
B (½)	10,000	20,000
		30,500

Thus in total, *A*'s share of profit amounts to £14,500 and *B*'s share to £16,000.

A separate set of accounts must be drawn up for tax purposes. Whilst the basic principles remain the same, certain items that are found in the firm's internal accounts as an expense are not deductible for tax purposes (eg depreciation of fixed assets, or a provision for doubtful debts). An adjustment would therefore have to be made by adding back these items, thus increasing the taxable profit. Similarly, there are certain items which would be deductible for tax purposes, but which would not appear in the internal accounts (eg claims in respect of capital allowances). Again a further adjustment would be necessary.

The balance sheet consists of a list of balances from the accounts at a stated date. The list is divided into assets and liabilities. The balance sheet equation is that assets = liabilities.

Example:
A and *B* start in partnership by both introducing £10,000 in capital; they agree that profits are to be shared equally. An accountant would consider the firm as separate from the partners, and therefore the capital belonging to the firm (asset) would be a debt owed to the partners (liability). Thus a simple balance sheet would show:

A & B Balance Sheet as at 1 January 198–

Liabilities		£	*Assets*	£
Capital accounts	*A*	10,000	Cash	20,000
	B	10,000		
		20,000		20,000

It is possible to adjust the assets side of the balance sheet without adjusting the liability side, by converting one asset into another.

Example:
If the above firm were to purchase premises for £10,000, and fixtures, fittings, and office machinery for £5,000, the balance sheet would look like this:

A & B Balance Sheet at as 1 January 198–

Liabilities		£	*Assets*	£
Capital accounts	*A*	10,000	*Fixed assets*	
	B	10,000	Premises	10,000
			Fixtures & fittings	5,000
			Current assets	
			Cash	5,000
		20,000		20,000

What about profit? How does this appear in the balance sheet? Accountants will base the accounts on an earnings basis (see p 116). The profits will therefore be made up of:

1 work billed and paid for;
2 work billed and unpaid;
3 work not as yet billed.

Thus it is possible from the accounts to indicate how this profit is made up.

Example:
Assume that during the year 1 January to 31 December 198– the above partnership made a profit of £12,000. This might be broken down as follows:

	£
Work in progress (ie unbilled work)	3,000
Debtors	4,000
Cash received and used for purchase of new office car	3,000
Cash received and used for purchase of books	1,000
Increase in cash	1,000
	12,000

Thus the profit can be described as a net increase in assets, and as such these items must be included in the balance sheet.

Example:

A & B Balance Sheet as at 31 December 198–

Assets	£
Fixed assets	
Premises	10,000
Fixtures and fittings	5,000
Car	3,000
Library	1,000

Current assets	
Work in progress	3,000
Debtors	4,000
Cash (£5,000 + £1,000)	6,000
	32,000

How is the profit reflected on the liability side of the balance sheet in order to keep the balance sheet equation? It must be remembered that the firm is working for its proprietors, and therefore any profit that it makes is owed to the proprietors. It can be recorded in a separate account maintained for each partner and called a current account. The balance on this account will then represent undrawn profits.

Example:

A & B Balance Sheet as at 31 December 198–

Liabilities	£
Capital accounts	
A	10,000
B	10,000
Current accounts	
A—share of profit	6,000
B—share of profit	6,000
	£32,000

Any profits withdrawn by the partners in the form of drawings will of course reduce the cash balance and also reduce the partners' current accounts (because the liability of the firm is thereby reduced). In the example it should be noted that although the partners are entitled to £6,000 each in profit, they cannot withdraw this without borrowing money, or otherwise increasing the cash at the bank.

One method of increasing the cash is to decrease the figures for work in progress and debtors. Thus by billing the work in progress this asset will be converted into debtors, and by a more enthusiastic method of reminding debtors to pay, ultimately the cash can be increased. It cannot be stressed sufficiently that the partners must keep a close watch on these three current assets, ie work in hand, debtors, and cash. If the first two are increasing the third is bound to decrease; staff and other expenses must be paid whether or not the partnership is receiving a cash return from its profits. The system of accounts which is chosen should therefore be one which will indicate these items to the partners on at least a monthly basis. From this monthly information the partners should be able to take such action as is required (including interim billing if necessary) to remedy a situation which can easily get out of hand.

A further indicator which can be obtained from the accounts is whether or not the firm has problems with liquidity. This is something else partners should watch for at monthly intervals. The basic test that can be carried out (the 'acid test') is whether liquid assets (defined as cash, debtors and other easily realisable current assets) cover current liabilities (ie those liabilities which fall for payment during the course of the following twelve months). The minimum requirement is for the liquid assets to be at least equal to the current liabilities; if this is not so the practice is said to be 'overtrading', and could be in a dangerous financial state.

One item in the current liabilities which should be noted is the partnership's liability for taxation. On the preceding year basis of assessment (see p 35) the partners' liability for tax in the current year is quite possibly based on the profits made up to two years ago. So long as the profits continue to rise each year, there should be sufficient surplus to pay the tax based on the lower profits. Problems arise when the profits fall; now the partners must pay tax out of current profits based on profits of the preceding year which are higher. If no tax reserve has been made, the chances of bankruptcy are high. The only proper course is to ensure that sufficient profits are set aside each year into a tax reserve so that the tax, when payable on those profits, can be paid from the reserve (see p 103).

For the sake of completeness, the modern form of presentation of a balance sheet (ie vertical form) is set out below.

Example:

A & B Balance Sheet as at 31 December 198–

	£	£
Employment of capital		
Fixed assets		19,000
Add current assets	14,000	
Less current liabilities	1,000	13,000
		32,000

Financed by	
Capital accounts	20,000
Current accounts	12,000
Long term liabilities	—
	32,000

5 Methods of costing

If the accounts show that the profits are falling in real terms (ie after any inflationary increase has been taken into account), or that the profits are otherwise unsatisfactory, it is necessary to look outside the accounts for the reason. It may be that important clients have been lost; it may be that the practice is overcharging and thus driving clients away, or alternatively that the practice is not charging enough to cover increased overheads.

If either of the last two apply to the firm, serious consideration should be given to a system of time costing. Even if profits are satisfactory the only sensible way in which to assess profits is by the use of such a system. As far as the legal profession is concerned, there are complex regulations which lay down the basis of charging for professional work. For non-contentious work (conveyancing, probate, etc) the two rules are the Solicitors' Remuneration Order 1972, and the Rules of the Supreme Court (Non-contentious Probate Costs) 1956. There is an argument that the 1972 Order has replaced the 1956 Rules, despite the fact that the Rules were not specifically revoked, but this does not cause too many problems since the factors to be taken into account are similar in both the Rules and the Order. These factors are:

1 the difficulty and complexity (or novelty) of the questions raised;
2 the skill, labour, specialised knowledge and responsibility involved;
3 the time spent;
4 the number and importance of the documents prepared or perused;
5 the place where the business was transacted;
6 the value of the property involved;
7 the importance of the matter to the client;
8 whether any land involved was registered.

Whilst it is specifically mentioned in point no 3, time is also important in deciding points nos 1, 2, 4 and 7. That is, the more difficult the matter, the longer it will take; the more documents perused or prepared the longer it will take, and the more important the matter is to the client, the quicker he may want it done. Consequently, although the bill must be prepared so that the charge is fair having regard to all these circumstances, time obviously plays a highly important part. A system which gives a solicitor access to the exact amount of chargeable hours spent on a client's behalf should therefore be invaluable.

Time-costing works like this. The total expenses of the firm should be assessed from last year's accounts (eg salaries to staff, general overheads, insurances, etc). These expenses should then be adjusted to take into account inflation. The partners should then decide upon notional salaries for themselves, that is how much they would expect to receive for the work that they do, perhaps by reference to solicitors of equivalent seniority working in industry or the Civil Service (although the Law Society in the third edition of their pamphlet *The Expense of Time* (1981) suggest a figure of £10,500 per partner outside London; £14,000 within London). A further sum should then be added to these notional salaries to include a fair return on the partners' capital which they have invested in the partnership, any pension contributions which are needed to put a partner in the same position as someone in pensionable employment, and a sum representing 'superprofit'. This last figure represents the return a partner is entitled to as a result of the risk he takes compared to receiving a monthly pay cheque, and is an important factor.

The number of fee earners in the firm must then be ascertained. These could be partners, legal executives, assistant solicitors, and articled clerks. These are the people who work for clients, rather than those members of staff who work for fee earners.

It is also necessary to work out the number of hours spent on clients' matters during a normal working year. A figure of 1,100 hours is usually taken as being reasonable. This represents 60% of the available working hours assuming a 35-hour working week. The rest of the time can be taken up by non-chargeable administrative matters, holidays, sickness, etc. With this information it is possible to ascertain the firm's expense rate. That is how much the firm needs to charge each hour that it is open in order to cover the necessary expenses. The firm's expense rate is then apportioned between the fee earners according to their seniority.

Example:
AB & Co consists of two partners, *A* (aged 55) and *B* (aged 35). The firm also employs two senior legal executives and an articled clerk.

The expenses for last year were as follows:

	£	£
General expenses	50,000	
Add inflation at say 10%	5,000	55,000
Partners' notional salaries		
A	14,000	
B	14,000	28,000
Interest on capital		
A	3,000	
B	2,000	5,000
Pension contribution		
A	4,000	
B	3,000	7,000
Superprofit		4,000
		99,000

$$\text{Firm's expense rate} = \frac{\text{Income required}}{\text{number of chargeable hours per year}}$$

$$= \frac{99{,}000}{1{,}100}$$

$$= £90 \text{ per hour}$$

The expense rate can then be apportioned between the fee earners, eg

	£
A	35 ph
B	30 ph
LE (1)	10 ph
LE (2)	10 ph
Art cl	5 ph
	90 ph

Once the individuals' hourly charging rates have been ascertained, it is up to the system to indicate to the fee earners how long they have spent on individual client's affairs. Perhaps this is the biggest disadvantage of such a scheme; fee earners must keep a detailed record of all time spent on a particular matter, whether it amounts to routine correspondence, telephone calls, or interviews with clients. Time sheets of each fee earner are completed each day and the information is fed into a central system (many such systems combine the facility of time costing with word processing). The advantages of using a more sophisticated system is that other information can be retrieved at regular intervals. If the machine has details of all time spent on all the clients' matters, it is very easy to assess the current level of work in hand. The partners at their regular monthly meetings can discuss this figure, and if it is too high can take the appropriate steps.

Two further points must be made concerning this system of time-costing. First, time is *not* the only factor to be taken into account; it is one of a number of factors. Whilst then a time costing system will give the basis upon which a solicitor can assess his client's bill, it is only the starting point. Care must be taken to adjust the figure according to the overall circumstances. Secondly, it is really only safe to apply these principles to the costing of non-contentious matters. The rules on costs and litigation are complex, and are not the subject of this book; the case of *R* v *Wilkinson* [1980] 1 All ER 597, is authority for the statement that this system of time-costing does not provide a reliable basis for the taxation of contentious costs. Subject, however, to these two provisos, time-costing can be an invaluable aid to the practitioner.

6 Taxation

(*a*) *Income tax*

Partnership income is subject to income tax. It is not, like company income, subject to corporation tax. Section 152 of the Income and Corporation Taxes Act 1970 provides:

> Where a trade or profession is carried on by two or more persons jointly, income tax in respect thereof shall be computed and stated jointly, and in one sum, and shall be separate and distinct from any other tax chargeable on those persons or any of them, and a joint assessment shall be made in the partnership name.

A partnership is taxed on its net profits computed in accordance with Schedule D depending on whether it is a trading partnership (Case I) or whether it is a professional partnership (Case II). Having calculated its gross profits, the firm will then deduct all allowable expenditure, eg rent, rates, salaries, and make further adjustments to take account of capital allowances, loss relief and stock or work in progress relief.

In calculating the receipts of the firm for the purpose of establishing the amount of taxable profit, the basis of accounting used is important. It is time, therefore, to look at this in more detail. When a firm starts, it will for the first three years, in any event, have to calculate its profits on what is known as the earnings basis of accounting. This means as we have seen, that work done, billed and paid for will be included, work done and billed will be included even though it has not been paid for, and work done but not yet billed (work in progress) will have to be included. Thus, it can be seen, the partnership may have to pay tax on money that it has not yet received. Work in progress (work that has not yet been billed) has to be valued. Although this is generally valued excluding the cost of partners' time, thereafter the valuation depends on the view of the individual inspector of taxes. Some inspectors value it at a nominal value, others insist on giving it its full value. Under the earnings basis the allowable expenditure is not just that actually expended, it also includes those sums where the obligation to pay has arisen. The advantage of the earnings basis is that it produces more realistic accounts. It reflects the amount of work done during a year and therefore is not subject to the paying habits of clients. In addition, the new form of stock relief (called work in progress relief in the context of a solicitors' partnership—the work in progress being the equivalent of stock in a trading firm) will be of benefit to professional firms.

The other bases of accounting are known as the conventional bases of accounting and are the cash basis and the bills delivered basis. The cash basis simply means that the profits of the firm are calculated on the basis of cash received less cash paid out. The disadvantage of this from the firm's point of view is that although it defers the showing of profits for tax purposes (an advantage) it does not give a true indication of what the firm has done during the year as it only shows which clients have paid during the year, possibly for work done some time before. However, a firm with an efficient system of time-costing ought to be able to work out very easily the level of work sustained during a year.

The bills delivered basis brings into the charge to tax those amounts for which bills have been delivered, and allows as deductions those amounts for which bills have been received. It thus excludes work in progress, but does include work done, billed, but not yet paid for. The Solicitors' Accounts Rules 1975 revolve round this method of accounting, and perhaps it is appropriate for solicitors who cannot recover their costs until a bill has been delivered.

As already stated the Revenue insist that the earnings basis be used at least for the first three years of the firm; thereafter they may allow a change to a conventional basis if the figure of profits, taking one year with another, is not substantially different from that calculated on an earnings basis. If the firm wishes to make the change, then it must give to the Revenue a written undertaking that it will issue bills regularly and frequently at specified intervals. If the firm is considering changing the basis of accounting, then the advantages and disadvantages should be carefully considered, eg that on a change from the earnings basis to cash basis, certain work may be brought into the charge to tax twice, once under the earnings basis if, eg, it was billed in the year in question but not paid for, and secondly under the cash basis in the next year, if that is the year in which the bill is actually paid.

The assessment to tax. The partnership is taxed on its profits on a preceding year basis. Thus, as previously explained, the profits of the accounting year ending in the previous year of assessment are the profits charged to tax in the present year of assessment. This rule does not apply in the opening years of a business (see p 35).

So that the Revenue can discover the level of profit in any one year, a return of partnership income has to be made. This is the duty of the 'precedent' partner. (Taxes Management Act 1970, s 9(1).) The precedent partner is the acting partner who is first named in the partnership agreement or who is first named in the firm name. Thus it is his responsibility to submit the accounts of the relevant accounting year with any necessary adjustments made specifically for tax purposes, eg in respect of capital allowances.

If the partnership as a whole had a separate legal identity as a company does, then the assessment to tax would be simple: the profits would be assessed to tax at x% being the appropriate rate of tax in the way that a company is taxed at 52% (or 40%) on its profits. However, since a partnership does not have an existence separate from the individuals who make up the partnership the assessment becomes much more complicated. The firm cannot be taxed; the individual partners have to be taxed. Each partner may receive a different share of the profits and bearing in mind the level of his partnership income, and the level of his personal reliefs (see p 30), the rate of tax applied to each partner's share of the profits may be different. To give an example: a partner who is single and lives in rented accommodation, will, if he receives £15,000 profit from the firm, only be able to set a single person's allowance of £1,565 against it. Thus he will be taxed on £13,435. The first £12,800 is taxed at 30% and the remainder at 40%. His total tax bill is £4,094. If another partner, receiving the same amount from the firm, is married and has a mortgage on which he makes interest repayments of £2,000 a year, then he will be taxed on £10,555 (he was able to deduct the mortgage interest and married man's allowance of £2,445). His total tax bill is £3,166·50. Therefore, in addition to the return of the partnership income made by the precedent partner, the individual partners also have to make a return of their income so that personal reliefs and charges on income can be applied and the amount of tax on each individual's share of the partnership income worked out. The sum of the individuals' tax is the amount of tax which the partnership has to pay. It should be remembered that the partnership is assessed to tax on a preceding year basis so that the partners are paying tax in the current year of assessment on profits earned in an earlier year of assessment.

There is, however, a further rule which adds to the complexity of partnership taxation. When deciding how much of the preceding year's profits to allocate to each individual partner so that liability to tax can be ascertained, the Revenue will, instead of merely dividing those profits as they were actually shared in that preceding year, divide them according to the current year's profit-sharing ratios. This causes no problem if profit-sharing ratios have not changed but can lead to a partner paying more than his fair share of tax in a year when his profit-sharing ratio has increased. For this reason it is usual to provide in the deed that on a change in profit-sharing ratios the other partners will indemnify a partner whose tax liability is higher than it would have otherwise been. The calculation of this additional liability can be a long and difficult process for it means that a partner will have to reveal his personal circumstances to the others for the purposes of working out how much tax he would have paid if the change had not come about.

Example

A and *B* are in partnership sharing profits equally. They make up their accounts to 31 December in each year. In April 1981 they admit *C* as a partner. Thereafter profits are to be shared as to *A* ⅓, *B* ⅓ and *C* ⅓.

The profits are as follows:

1.1.80–31.12.80 = £55,000
1.1.81–31.12.81 = £60,000

During the calendar year 1981 the profit will be shared as follows:
3 months (1.1.81–31.3.81)

	£		£
A (½)	7,500	Apportioned profit (3/12 × 60,000)	15,000
B (½)	7,500		
	15,000		15,000

9 months (1.4.81–31.12.81)

	£		£
A (⅓)	15,000	Apportioned profit (9/12 × 60,000)	45,000
B (⅓)	15,000		
C (⅓)	15,000		
	45,000		45,000

For the *tax year* 1981–82 (when the bulk of 1981's profits are made) the tax bill will be assessed on the preceding year basis, ie the firm's statutory income for 1981–82 will be £55,000. *C* therefore as a partner during the tax year will find himself paying tax on the basis of his current profit-sharing ratio (ie ⅓) on income which he has never received and which was earned *before* he became a partner (ie £55,000). In the tax year 1982–83 he will pay tax on the profit made during the accounting year ending 31 December 1981. He should therefore seek an indemnity from his fellow partners.

Interest on capital and salaries. As has already been pointed out, interest on capital and salaries are merely different ways of adjusting the profit-sharing ratios. By salaries, we mean those that are a first charge on the profits and are paid to full equity partners, rather than those which are paid to 'salaried partners'. The Revenue allocate the preceding year's profits according to this year's profit-sharing ratios; as interest and salaries are part of the profits they apply exactly the same principle and take into account interest and any salary actually paid in the current year of assessment. Effectively, the Revenue work on all the information that is available about the current year—interest, salary and profit-sharing ratios. The one piece of current information that is not available is the level of profit, for the accounts will not yet have been made up, and so the preceding year's profit figure has to be used.

Example:
X, *Y* and *Z* share profits in the following ratios. *X*—a salary of £1,000; *Y*—interest on capital of £500 and a salary of £750; *Z*—interest on capital of £750. Thereafter, the balance is split equally. Their accounts are made up to 31 December each year.

Their appropriation account for the year ending 31 December 1980 is:

	£	£		£
Interest on capital			*Profit*	21,000
Y	500			
Z	750	1,250		
Salaries				
X	1,000			
Y	750	1,750		

	£	£		£
Balance				
X	6,000			
Y	6,000			
Z	6,000	18,000		
		21,000		21,000

Thus for the year ending 31 December 1980 *X*'s entitlement is £7,000 (1,000+6,000); *Y*'s entitlement is £7,250 (500 + 750 + 6,000); *Z*'s entitlement is £6,750 (750 + 6,000).

The £21,000 is the firm's statutory income for the tax year 1981–82. If the partners decide to change their profit shares on 6 April 1981 and the profits are shared as to *X*—a salary of £2,500; *Y*—interest on capital of £250 and a salary of £2,500; *Z*—interest on capital of £750; the balance shared equally, the statutory income of £21,000 will be taxed in the proportion to which the partners share profits in 1981–82. Thus for tax purposes:

	£	£		£
Interest on capital			*Statutory income*	21,000
Y	250			
Z	750	1,000		
Salaries				
X	2,500			
Y	2,500	5,000		
Balance				
X	5,000			
Y	5,000			
Z	5,000	15,000		
		21,000		21,000

The position is therefore that *X*'s entitlement was £7,000 but he is taxed on £7,500; *Y*'s entitlement was £7,250 but he is taxed on £7,750; *Z*'s entitlement was £6,750 but he is taxed on £5,750.

When calculating the amount of profit that the firm has made, it should be stressed that interest on capital and payment of a salary to a profit-sharing partner are not deductible expenses; it should also be realised that even if the partners do not draw all their profit out of the firm but leave some in their current accounts to provide working capital, they will nevertheless be taxed on it.

Payment of tax. The assessment to tax is made on the partnership but it can either be paid out of the partnership account or by the individual partners out of their own bank accounts. The liability of the partners is joint, which means that in the event of the firm failing to pay the tax bill, or an individual failing to pay his part of the tax bill, another partner could be made to pay the whole or a large proportion of the tax bill out of his own private estate. He would of course have the right to seek an indemnity from the other partners for any sums so paid.

The firm's income tax liability is paid in two equal instalments. The first falls due on 1 January in the year of assessment, and the second on 1 July following. Interest on unpaid tax is chargeable from the date that payment is due (1 January or 1 July) or from thirty days after the date of assessment. The assessment will also include the partners' liabilities for Class 4 National Insurance contributions.

Whether the tax is paid by the partners individually, or by the firm, it is of the utmost importance to give thought to how the bill is to be met. In advising anyone who is being taxed under Schedule D for the first time, rather than Schedule E, it is essential to point out that provision must be made for the two lump sum payments of tax. A person who is used to receiving his money net of tax under the PAYE scheme (under Schedule E) may not at first appreciate the dangers of drawing money gross out of the firm. If he spends all that he draws from the firm, and draws all of his profits out of the firm, then neither he nor the firm will have the cash with which to pay the Revenue. Although in some partnerships it may be the wish of the individual partners that they pay their own share of the tax bill, it is more usual, and a better course of action, for the firm to pay the tax. If this is the case, the firm must consider how it is going to meet the payments. One of the ways in which this can be done is to ensure that partners do not draw all of their share of the profit out of the firm, but leave a proportion of the profits in the firm to create a tax reserve. Another way in which this can be done is to meet the tax bill by short term borrowing from the bank. Whether this will be necessary depends on the overall profitability of the firm in the current year and also any cash flow problems the firm may have—how quickly and how often it is billing its clients. 1 January is a particularly difficult date, however, and some borrowing may be necessary (see p 103).

(*b*) *Capital gains tax*

On setting up a partnership no capital gains tax problems arise. However, during the course of the firm's existence CGT problems may arise either when chargeable assets are sold by the firm, or when there is some change in the firm itself, either because profit-sharing ratios change between existing partners or because a new partner joins the firm or one leaves the firm. The latter two points will be dealt with at a later stage (see pp 144 and 153).

Capital gains tax is payable on the disposal of a chargeable asset, always assuming that a gain is made; if it is not the capital loss can be set against other gains (see p 41). Where a professional partnership is concerned the main chargeable asset is likely to be the freehold or leasehold premises in which the firm carries on business. Another important and chargeable asset is the goodwill of the firm—if this increases in value and is disposed of, a capital gain has been made. Most of the other capital assets of the firm are likely to be tangible movable property which is a wasting asset and therefore exempt from CGT, eg the office machinery; in addition cars are exempt from CGT. The painting of the founder of the firm by a famous nineteenth century artist or the Chippendale boardroom table and set of twelve matching chairs will also be chargeable assets and subject to CGT if the firm disposes of them.

For CGT to be chargeable there has to be a disposal. Disposal is usually by sale or gift. To calculate the gain the acquisition or base cost (ie what it cost to acquire the asset plus any expenses of acquiring it, and anything spent on it since to improve it) is set against the consideration received on the disposal (subject to the index linking provisions of the Finance Act 1982). If the asset is sold, the consideration will be the sale price. If the asset is given away or sold at much less than its true value, then the Revenue may substitute market value and calculate the gain on that on the grounds that the asset was disposed of other than by way of a bargain made at arm's length. Transfers between 'connected persons' are deemed to be otherwise than by way of a bargain at arm's length unless the price is freely negotiated. Persons are connected persons if they fall within the definition in s 63 of the Capital Gains Tax Act 1979. A person and his or her spouse, relative or spouse of a relative are connected persons. Relative means brother, sister, ancestor or lineal descendant. Except in relation to acquisitions or disposals of partnership assets pursuant to bona fide commercial arrangements, a person is connected with any person with whom he is in partnership, and with the husband or wife or a relative of any individual with whom he is in partnership. Thus the Revenue will substitute market value where there is a gift between connected persons, but it should be remembered that any gain so calculated can be held over until the donee disposes of the asset (Finance Act 1980, s 79: see p 44).

Any gain made on the disposal of a partnership asset is not

treated by the Revenue as a gain of the firm, but it is treated as a gain made by the individual partners. How is this gain calculated? Each partner is treated as owning a fractional share in the partnership assets. When a disposal is made each partner has allocated to him a part of the acquisition cost and a part of the consideration received on disposal. The allocations are made according to the ratio of shares in the asset surpluses at the relevant time. Asset surpluses means capital profits. Partners share capital profits in the same way as they share income profits unless it is otherwise agreed (see p 79). These rules can be found in the Inland Revenue Statement of Practice of 17 January 1975 which is set out in Appendix 2. They are not contained in the Capital Gains Tax legislation because it seems the application of the legislation to partnerships was forgotten by the draftsmen. For general rules therefore the Capital Gains Tax Act 1979 must be consulted, but for their particular application to partnership the Revenue Statement of Practice and any later amendments to it must be considered.

Disposal of a chargeable asset to an outsider. Suppose a firm sells its freehold premises for £100,000 having bought it for £70,000 (including expenses). The firm consists of two partners sharing profits equally; *A* contributed £20,000 towards the purchase of the property and *B* contributed £10,000 (part of their capital contributions). When the property is sold a £30,000 gain is made. This gain has to be allocated to the individual partners to discover whether any and if so how much CGT must be paid. The acquisition cost is shared in the same way as they shared asset surpluses at the time: as the partners shared profits equally and have not agreed otherwise, they share asset surpluses equally (see Partnership Act 1890, s 24). It makes no difference that they contributed different amounts of capital to the firm. They will take that out of the firm on leaving; it is only the capital profits that we are concerned with. The acquisition cost is thus £35,000 each.

On disposal the consideration received is set against the acquisition cost, having first been allocated according to asset surplus sharing ratios. In this example the ratios have not changed so the consideration is shared equally: each partner therefore receives £50,000 and each has thus made a gain of £15,000. As the first £5,000 gain in any year is exempt from CGT then, providing no other gains have been made during the year, each will pay CGT on £10,000 at 30%, ie each will pay £3,000 CGT.

If, however, the reason for selling was to buy new and perhaps bigger premises and if all of the consideration on the sale is put towards the acquisition of new premises then roll-over relief will be available (see Capital Gains Tax Act 1979, s 115) and no CGT will be paid until the premises are finally disposed of without being replaced.

Disposal of a chargeable asset to a partner. Let us imagine that the firm's premises were a small, but very desirable, Georgian house in the town. The firm needs to move to more modern offices but instead of selling them to an outsider the firm sells to one of the partners who decides (subject of course to planning permission) to live in the house. Partner *B* is the partner who is to live in the house; he is prepared to pay £50,000 to partner *A*.

As far as partner *A* is concerned, the position is just the same as it was in the first example. What about partner *B*? He has disposed of his half share in a partnership asset to himself as an individual. He has made a £15,000 gain on this disposal to himself. However, because he has received no money for this disposal, the gain is held over until he finally disposes of the property. When he finally does the gain will be calculated thus: Acquisition cost £50,000 (from *A*) + £35,000 (£50,000 − the gain of £15,000 held over) = £85,000. This will be set against whatever he receives for the property to find the gain.

If that boardroom table and set of chairs were disposed of to a partner they might be given to him or sold to him for much less than their true cost (having been written down to a very low valuation in the accounts). If that were the case the Revenue would be able to substitute market value as the consideration received as the disposal would be between connected persons and otherwise than at arm's length. In addition, it could be argued that *A* had by giving the table and chairs to *B*, or selling them for less than their true value, reduced the value of his estate thereby incurring capital transfer tax liability.

Change in profit-sharing ratios. If it is remembered that partners are taken as sharing partnership assets in the same ratio as they share profits, it is not difficult to understand that if partners change profit-sharing ratios so also do they change asset surplus sharing ratios (ie capital profit-sharing ratios). In our example, if, having up till now shared profits equally, *A* is to have 2/3rds of the profits and *B* is to have 1/3rd, then *B*'s share of the asset surpluses has gone down as well as his share of the profits. He has in fact *disposed* of a 1/6th share in the asset surpluses. He might have done this because, eg, he has reached an age where he wishes to take a lesser part in the running of the firm. Let us continue working on the basis that the firm's only chargeable asset is the freehold premises, this time bought for £72,000 and now worth £120,000. On the face of it, *B* appears to have made the following gain when he disposes to *A* his 1/6th share in the asset surplus:

Acquisition cost of *B*'s share of premises	= £36,000
Thus, acquisition cost of 1/6th share	= £12,000
Present value of whole of *B*'s share	= £60,000
Value of 1/6th share on disposal	= £20,000
Apparent gain	= £8,000

The words apparent gain are used because, in practice, it is unlikely that *B* will have actually made a gain as *A* will not have paid for the increased share. On a change in asset surplus-sharing ratios, consideration will be balance sheet value plus any cash paid between the partners or market value if the disposal was not at arm's length (Inland Revenue Statement of Practice, 17 January 1975: see Appendix 2).

Thus if *A* pays *B* for his increased share, *B* will have made a gain and suffer capital gains tax liability; if the asset is revalued upwards and no longer appears at its original balance sheet value, *B* will also have made a gain and be liable to CGT on the disposal of his share. If, however, there is no revaluation and no cash changes hands, then *B* has disposed of his share at the same price as he acquired it and thus has made no gain. However, as we have already seen, the Revenue can substitute market value in this situation if they feel that the transaction was not at arm's length. On the face of it, it is not at arm's length because it is between 'connected persons', ie partners. Substitution of market value can, however, be avoided by showing that there is no gift because there has been a bona fide commercial transaction ie that the acquiring partner is providing some consideration for his increased share, eg he is taking an increased share of the work load. (For cases on bona fide commercial transactions see *Att-Gen* v *Boden* [1912] 1 KB 539 and *Att-Gen* v *Ralli* (1936) 15 ATC 523.)

If in fact, the disposal really is a gift because, let us say, *A* is the son of *B*, then the Revenue will substitute market value and assess *B* on the gain he is deemed to have made. Then it may be necessary to elect for hold-over relief under the Finance Act 1980, s 79. If this election is made, CGT will not have to be paid now: liability will be deferred until such time as *A* disposes of his share. If *B* is assessed to capital gains tax on the gain of £8,000 that he has made or is deemed to have made, then the availability of any reliefs should be considered. In these circumstances the first £5,000 of any gain will be exempt.

Everything that has been said on a change in profit and thus asset surplus sharing ratios between existing partners applies equally when a new partner enters the firm (see p 144).

(*c*) *Capital transfer tax*

As was seen in Part I, CTT becomes relevant when there is a transfer of value which is not at arm's length and is not for market value, which thus reduces the value of the transferor's estate. Where a partnership is concerned it may become relevant wherever there is a gift element in any changing of asset surplus ratios. However, as a general rule for reasons which will be explained, CTT does not cause many problems in the context of a partnership.

In the context of an existing firm, the danger area will be that which we have recently discussed in relation to CGT, ie where there is a change in profit-sharing and thus asset surplus sharing ratios. If there is no consideration for the transfer then there has been a gift by the transferor and his estate has diminished in value (in the example on p 125 *B* has given 1/6th share to *A*). Prima facie therefore there is liability to CTT. However, this may be avoided if the arrangement falls within s 20(4) of the Finance Act 1975—what is known as the non-gratuitous arm's length exemption. Under this subsection it is possible to claim that the arrangements are part of a bona fide commercial bargain made without gratuitous intent. If therefore the partner acquiring an increased share does so while at the same time agreeing to do more work in the firm, then s 20(4) would appear to be satisfied. To ensure that this is so, it is advisable to draft a partnership deed or to alter an existing deed so that this covenant will appear. Alternatively the partner disposing of part of his share might have done so in return for better pension arrangements to be provided by the remaining partners. Again this should satisfy the commercial bargain test for both CGT and CTT.

When a new partner enters a firm, when goodwill is abolished or when a partner dies or retires, CTT may become relevant. See pp 145; 90; and 156 respectively.

7 Employees

Most professional partnerships will at some time need to employ staff, and consequently the partners must be made aware of the law relating to employees. The principal duties of an employer are as follows:

(1) To pay wages. Payment must be without deduction (except for PAYE income tax, national insurance deductions and other deductions consented to by the employee).

(2) Providing the employee has worked for at least four weeks, to provide him with a written statement containing the major terms of his employment contract in accordance with s 1 of the Employment Protection (Consolidation) Act 1978. This statement must be received by the employee not later than thirteen weeks after the employment began and must contain the following details: identification of the parties; date when employment began and whether any previous employment counts as part of the employee's continuous period of employment; rates of pay and interval when paid; hours of work; holiday entitlement; sickness pay entitlement; details of pension schemes; length of notice required to terminate the contract of employment; job title; and disciplinary rules applicable to the employee.

(3) To take reasonable care for his employees' safety.

(4) To indemnify the employee against all liability and expense incurred by him in the proper performance of his work. There is also a duty on the employee to indemnify the employer against liability incurred as a result of an employee's failure to exercise reasonable skill and care in performing his duties. This could mean that an employee of a firm of solicitors who by his negligence or lack of reasonable care puts his employers into a position where they are liable in negligence to a third party could be required to indemnify his employer against the consequent loss sustained. This, however, is extremely rare in practice since such loss would invariably be covered by indemnity insurance. Two further points must be made. First, there is usually an excess clause in the insurance policy which will require the insured to pay out the first specified amount of the claim. This excess could presumably be claimed from the defaulting employee. Secondly, in theory, the insurance company having paid the claim could themselves seek an indemnity from the employee by use of the doctrine of subrogation. With regard to the compulsory insurance required by solicitors under the Solicitors' Indemnity Rules 1975–81, the insurers have indicated that they would be unlikely to pursue such a claim.

Having employed the members of staff in accordance with such statutory and common law duties, the second problem area relates to the dismissal of such employees. The termination of contracts of employment has become a vast and complex area of law. Most of the law has now been consolidated into the Employment Protection (Consolidation) Act 1978 as amended by the Employment Act 1980. The area neatly divides into two possible statutory claims and a common law claim.

There are common conditions to be satisfied for the two statutory claims for redundancy payments and unfair dismissal. These are first, that the applicant must be an employee and secondly, he must have been dismissed in accordance with the definition of dismissal to be found in the 1978 Act. Broadly dismissal will either be satisfied when the employer terminates the contract with or without notice, or where a fixed term contract expires without being renewed, or where the employer by his conduct repudiates the contract, and this repudiation is accepted by the employee's resignation (ie constructive dismissal). From a partner's point of view it should be noted that s 142 of the 1978 Act as amended allows an employee to contract out of protection against unfair dismissal or a redundancy payment where there is a fixed term contract, and the dismissal occurs on the expiry of the term without renewal. For exclusion of unfair dismissal rights the fixed term must be for one year or more; for exclusion of redundancy rights the fixed term must be for two years or more. Consequently partners should consider, when employing staff, whether a fixed term contract should be given, linked with an exclusion term which should be embodied in the contract.

A further condition to be satisfied in respect of a statutory claim is continuous employment for the relevant period. The relevant period for a claim for unfair dismissal is fifty-two weeks; for redundancy payments, two years. Consequently dismissals of employees who have insufficient service will not give rise to a statutory claim. A further important concession has been given to employers whose employees do not exceed twenty in number. In such a case the Employment Act 1980 has extended the period of qualification for a claim in respect of unfair dismissal to a period in excess of two years. This is particularly helpful, for example, to partnerships which are starting from scratch and where the partners do not wish to be unduly concerned about employees making claims during the infancy of the firm.

If an employer has to dismiss an employee who does qualify for protection it is still open to the employer to prove the dismissal fair.

If a claim is made to an industrial tribunal, the employer needs to show that the reason or principal reason for dismissal was either the conduct of the employee; redundancy; that it would be illegal to continue to employ the employee; the capability or qualifications of the employee; or some other substantial reason justifying dismissal. Further the tribunal must satisfy itself that in the circumstances the employer acted reasonably in treating this reason as the reason for dismissal.

In a claim for redundancy payments, there is a presumption that the dismissal was by reason of redundancy, so it is up to the employer to prove otherwise. Although the average award of compensation is not high, it is open to a firm to insure against the possibility of having to pay such compensation. The present maximum compensation which can be awarded is £18,070 with effect from 1 February 1982, but this figure will rarely if ever be awarded. Where a firm is forced to make a redundancy payment (which is based on the employee's age, length of service, and week's pay) a rebate, at present 41%, can be claimed from the Secretary of State for Employment, such rebate being paid from the redundancy fund. The maximum amount of payment is at present £4,050.

The common law claim which can be made is for wrongful dismissal, and in most cases firms should be able to avoid such claims by ensuring that any dismissal is carried out strictly in accordance with the contractual terms (ie as to notice period, disciplinary procedure, etc).

Finally, many partnerships will employ married women who may exercise their right to maternity pay and maternity leave. To qualify for these rights, the employee must have been employed until the start of the eleventh week before the expected date of confinement and as at that date have been employed for at least two years. She must at least twenty-one days before her absence begins inform the employer that she will be absent by reason of pregnancy or confinement, and, if she wishes to return to work, that she so intends. By s 34 of the 1978 Act maternity pay is payable by the employer for six weeks from the date the employee leaves work and is nine-tenths of the employee's last weekly wage, less any maternity allowance payable. The employer claims a full rebate from the Secretary of State. If the employee intends to return to work she can on giving the appropriate notice return at any time before the end of the twenty-ninth week after the actual week of confinement. She must be employed in basically the same job as before and on equally favourable terms provided it is reasonable for the employer to comply with those terms. Failure on behalf of the employer to allow the employee to return may amount to dismissal which could give rise to the appropriate statutory claim.

Chapter 9

Expanding the Firm

1 The new partner

(a) Salaried partners

It is now fairly common for a partner to be appointed as a salaried partner as the first step towards becoming a full partner. A salaried partner is a halfway house between being an employee and a full profit-sharing partner. It is often used by firms to prevent really able assistant solicitors leaving to set up on their own or join a rival firm.

The salaried partner will usually be described on the firm's letterhead as a partner, and will also be so described to the rest of the outside world. He is thus not only likely to be holding himself out to be a partner but is also knowingly allowing himself to be held out as a partner. Under the doctrine of holding out (as to which see s 14 of the Partnership Act and p 19) he could therefore be liable for some of the firm's contract debts. However, with reference to the firm itself he is not likely to be a true partner. He will not be receiving a share of the profits and will not have put any capital into the firm. He will still be receiving a salary and will probably receive it net of tax under the PAYE system. Thus from the point of view of his financial interest in the firm, it is no different from what it was when he was an assistant solicitor. If he is still in the position of an employee then he continues to be subject to the current employment protection legislation, and also is not yet liable for the firm's income tax assessment. He is unlikely to have much control over the management of the firm; indeed if he were to take a full part in the management of the firm this might point towards him being a full partner.

It seems therefore, and indeed this was the view of Megarry J in *Stekel* v *Ellice* [1973] 1 WLR 191, that the term can embrace various possibilities: first, a partner by holding out but still an employee in the firm; secondly, a true partner both with regard to outsiders and the firm itself thus having a proprietary interest in the firm; thirdly, a 'qualified partner' who has some rights but not complete rights within the partnership. This latter was the case in *Stekel* v *Ellice* where the salaried partner was paid a fixed amount but not under the PAYE system, where he was a partner by holding out and a partner with regard to the rest of the firm except that having no proprietary interest it was held that he had no right to have the partnership wound up and the assets distributed.

The employee achieving the status of salaried partner should ensure that he understands the implications of his status. As he may be liable for some of the firm's debts but is unlikely to be taking any part in the management of the firm, it would be sensible and fair for him to be given an indemnity in respect of such debts.

This indemnity should be included in the salaried partnership agreement which should be drawn up. In addition to the indemnity the agreement should make it clear that the salaried partner is required to contribute no capital and shall not be liable for any losses of the firm. It is likely to state that the salaried partner is not entitled to take part in the control or management of the practice, or if the salaried partner is to be allowed some decision-making power, the agreement will define this. In addition the agreement will lay down the terms on which the salaried partner works for the firm, his salary, holiday, period of notice, etc.

If the partnership is one of solicitors, any salaried partner whose name is on the headed notepaper is being held out to the public as a partner for the purposes of the Solicitors' Indemnity Rules 1975–81. A premium must accordingly be paid.

(*b*) *The incoming partner*

Whilst the existing partners will want to know much about their prospective new partner before he is brought into the firm, he or she should want to find out as much as possible about the firm and the terms of entry. The existing partners will obviously be interested in the new partner's experience and expertise and whether his particular field of practice will balance with theirs. They will want to know something about his personal life and the incoming partner should not be surprised to be asked questions about it. The nature of partnership is such both on a personal and a financial level that the parties must be able to work together and to trust each other. The new partner's age is also important because a firm which is to continue, which is to be able to pay to the retiring partners their share of capital and possibly an annuity, must have some partners left in it to carry on. A firm consisting of partners of the same age will in the long term create problems for itself because all the partners will wish to increase their profits at the same time, decrease the amount of work they do at the same time, and retire at the same time.

The incoming partner has many questions to ask too. Of course, if he has been in the firm as an assistant solicitor he will have some but by no means all of the answers. Some of the enquiries that might be made are examined below.

The firm. What type of firm is it? First, enquiry should be made as to the partners. How many are there, what type of partner, what are their ages? In the same way as the existing partners want to make sure that the incoming partner is the right person for them, the incoming partner should make sure that they are the right people for him. After all, he may be bound by the terms in the partnership deed to commit at least three years of his life to the firm (depending on the duration clause) and he does not want these years to be wasted ones. The number of partners will be important because in a firm where there are few, the incoming partner may be expected to be more of a general practitioner than a specialist. In a larger firm, there is likely to be more specialisation. If there is another partner in that particular department, then the incoming partner should investigate what responsibility he will be able to take and, for the ambitious, whether he will be able to have the full responsibility for that department before he is in his dotage. Here the age of the existing partner becomes relevant. The ages of all the partners are important. The incoming partner may suspect, if both of the two existing partners for example are in their late fifties or early sixties, that he is being brought in to earn sufficient to provide for their retirement. Are there any consultants or sleeping partners? Usually a consultant will work in return for his consultancy fee, or in any event the fact that he is still associated with the firm will be of benefit to it, provided of course he has a high reputation rather than a low one. 'Sleeping partners' are not a separate legal type of partner; the term is more a term of endearment or perhaps criticism. A sleeping partner leaves the running of the firm, and the work of the firm, to others but is still liable as a partner. Provided this does not lead to too great a drain on the firm's resources, it may be no problem.

In a larger firm there will be senior and junior partners, with the former taking a greater part in the firm's management. The new partner is likely to be coming in at a junior level and should be sure exactly what that means and whether he is satisfied with the position he will hold in the firm. The type of work that the firm does is also important. Will there be sufficient scope for the incoming partner to realise his potential, whatever that may be?

The firm's finances. The incoming partner must investigate the financial position of the firm. It is after all on this that his future depends. Whilst a difficult financial situation may not inevitably deter him (he may after all be able to put the firm back on its feet by his own efforts), he should think very carefully about joining such a firm. As well as asking questions of the existing partners, the accounts of the firm should be studied. The existing partners should not be surprised if the incoming partner asks to see the last three years' accounts at least; indeed they should put this down as a mark in his favour.

From the accounts various matters can be discovered. First, the capital structure of the firm can be identified. The Remuneration Survey of the Law Society showed that in many firms the capital was provided by the older partners. If this is so, it creates great problems for the junior partners when the older ones retire. If there is a large amount of fixed capital in the firm (let us say that the firm owns two sets of office premises), then the retiring partners may need to be paid for their share in this. A look at the partnership deed may show whether this is to be by a lump sum or by instalments, and whether it is to be based on balance sheet value (which may never have been brought up to date) or whether on market value (which will include recent increases in property values).

How is the working capital provided? Again the accounts will give a lot of information on this. A look at the state of the partners' current accounts will show whether they draw out all of their entitlement to profit, or whether some is left in to fund working capital requirements. Does the firm rely heavily on bank borrowing? The accounts will show whether the current bank account is heavily overdrawn and if they give an indication of extensive long-term borrowing further questions should be asked about this.

The net profit of the firm over the past few years should be compared. If it is going up, this may look satisfactory but it may only be keeping pace with inflation. If it has not even kept pace with inflation then again questions should be asked. This may be due to the fact that over the past few years conveyancing has contracted in volume; the new partner is being brought in to develop another department which with his or her skill and effort will increase profitability. If overheads have increased substantially, this may be because salaries or rents have gone shooting up. It might point towards the fact that the firm relies too heavily on employees and not enough on modern technology. The existing partners cannot of course be forced to change their ways, but once in the firm the new partner can bear this in mind. Of course if the firm is under-equipped and there are plans to change this, remember that the capital cost of the machinery or the leasing costs will have to be met.

A study of the partners' drawings will show whether money is left in the firm to provide working capital and whether any provision is made for the tax bill. If there is a partner on the same or a similar share of the profits as that projected for the incoming partner, it will be interesting to see whether he is expected to leave money in the firm and to consider whether it will be possible to meet all commitments out of projected drawings.

If work in progress is excluded then current debtors should at least be able to meet current liabilities and ideally should exceed liabilities by 50%. This is calculated on the basis that if all creditors turned up on the firm's doorstep one morning, so also would all the firm's debtors! The level of work in progress and debtors can be ascertained from the accounts and this will give an idea as to the firm's approach to its billing and collection of sums owed.

All of this is discoverable from looking at the accounts and asking questions of the partners. An incoming partner who does not feel able to interpret the accounts sufficiently well should ask if he can show them to an accountant for his view of them. The incoming partner should not feel reticent about this, after all if he were merely buying shares in a public company he would have a lot of this information available; how much more important is it when his whole future is at stake. The incoming partner should not panic at the first unsatisfactory matter he comes across and refuse to join the firm; many problems are temporary, explainable, or will in the end be remedied. It is just that he should have all the information available to make what is a very important decision in his life.

The incoming partner's position in the firm. There are many aspects to be considered from the points of view of all parties. Assuming that if the terms are right all parties are agreed that the new partner should join the firm, then other matters will have to be decided and negotiated. First, when is the new partner going to join the firm? From an accounting point of view the best date to join is likely to be at the end of the accounting year/tax year. Secondly, the duration of the relationship should be considered. If it is to be a partnership at will, then any of the partners can bring the firm to an end without notice. If it is not a partnership at will, then should there be any provision for a partner leaving before retirement or death? It is probably sensible to include a provision that a partner can leave the firm on giving, eg, six months' notice, and that this does not dissolve the firm with regard to the remaining partners. In this way, a partner can leave to join another firm, to change careers, or because of ill health, without having to dissolve the whole firm and, if there is an accompanying clause on how he is to be paid his share of the assets, without destroying the financial base of the firm. When a new partner joins, an agreement that he should remain with the firm for at least, eg, three years can be made. In this way, he is required to devote at least a certain amount of his time to the firm whatever initial difficulties may be encountered.

The incoming partner should be advised as to whether he takes over the existing liabilities of the firm when he becomes a partner. Section 17(1) of the Partnership Act provides that 'A person who is admitted as a partner into an existing firm does not thereby become liable to the creditors of the firm for anything done before he became a partner.' It is usual to include a clause in the partnership deed to this effect. The existing partners agree to discharge all liabilities and debts of the former practice and to indemnify the incoming partner against all such debts and liabilities. As might be expected, with this clause usually goes another which allows the existing partners to have first claim to any money earned before the new partner joins the firm. A difficulty arises in the case of a continuing account with a customer or client, eg an overdrawn bank account. The new firm may continue to use this account in the same way as the old. When money is paid in, does it pay off the old or the new firm's debts? The rules in *Clayton's Case* (*Devaynes* v *Noble, Clayton's Case* (1816) 1 Mer 572) establish that anything paid towards satisfying the continuing debt pays off earlier liabilities first; debts are cancelled in chronological order. Once the old firm's debts have been paid off, the creditor cannot sue the members of the old firm. The only way a new partner can become liable for the old firm's debts is by what is known as a contract of novation (see s 17(3)). For this to happen, there must be an agreement, express or inferred from a course of dealings, between the old partners (including any retiring partner) the new partner and the creditor.

If the new partner is asked to sign the election for continuance for tax purposes then he may find himself with a heavier tax burden than he might otherwise have had; to compensate for this the existing partners will agree to indemnify him for this heavier burden (see p 142).

One of the main questions which the incoming partner may want answered is how and how much am I going to get paid? There are two possibilities: first he may be paid by way of a share in the profits, secondly, he may be paid a fixed salary by way of a first charge on the profits. He might even be paid by a combination of both a fixed salary and then a smaller share of the remaining profits. The advantage of a salary is that he will know what he will receive as a minimum amount. This may be important, bearing in mind his outgoings. He may have mortgage repayments to make, he may be required to leave money in his current account to go towards his capital contribution and the tax reserve; or he may alternatively be required to borrow to produce his capital and there will be repayments to be made here. In addition the partnership deed may require him to enter into pension arrangements. What all this amounts to is that in negotiating his financial position he must be aware of his own personal cash flow problems. While considering the advantages that partnership may eventually produce, ie a large share of a successful firm's profits, he may find that his financial position (particularly bearing in mind the new outgoings) is not as satisfactory as it was when he was an employee. All this of course has to be weighed up in making the decision. The new partner will also be interested in whether the firm is prepared to provide him with any 'perks' particularly in the form of a car. He will want to know whether the firm has a good car scheme as it is unlikely that he will be able to afford to buy a good car himself.

Retirement. Even at this early stage in his career, the new partner should have some thought as to what is to happen on his retirement. First, he must consider his pension arrangements. A pension can be provided in one of two ways: either the firm can pay him one by way of annuity instead of a repayment of capital and/or capital profits and goodwill (this is more fully discussed in the next chapter) or, and this is more satisfactory, he can purchase a pension through a retirement annuity scheme. Indeed, he may be required to enter into such a scheme by the terms of the partnership deed. It is advisable for a deed to stipulate this for then partners know that they will not be faced with the burden of providing a pension for an outgoing partner out of their own profits. If he is entering the partnership at a young age he may not have to enter a scheme until later—the deed might make it a requirement that he join the scheme at, eg, thirty-five years of age (for a discussion of retirement annuity contracts and tax relief claimable see p 91). The second matter he must consider at this early stage is how he is going to be paid his capital share on retirement; whether goodwill is an asset appearing in the balance sheet and whether this should continue; if part of his capital relates to fixed assets are these going to be valued at book or market value on retirement; and whether he will take some part of his capital in the form of an annuity, or as a lump sum payable forthwith or by instalments. These matters are for consideration and negotiation and if he is joining an established firm which has a partnership deed which covers them, it is likely that he will have to agree to the existing provisions in the deed.

The capital contribution of the new partner. The new partner will be required to contribute capital. This is necessary for a number of different reasons. As we have seen, a firm always needs working capital and if the firm is expanding with the advent of the new partner then so also will its working capital requirements be expanding. The new partner will need office space, office furniture and equipment, a secretary and so on. If the firm possesses fixed assets, then as we have seen (p 124) when the new partner enters the firm and takes a share of the profits, he also immediately has a right to a similar share in the asset surpluses unless the contrary is expressed. If the assets have not been revalued (with consequent CGT implications) then he immediately takes a share in profits that have been accruing over years when he was not a partner. The existing partners may want compensating for this in the form of some capital payment. The firm may be one which still values goodwill as an asset and again, as this has been built up by the existing partners and not by the new one, the former may want payment for this (by way of a payment for goodwill, as distinguished from capital). Another reason for the introduction of capital, and one which the incoming partner should be wary of, is that the introduction of new capital is the only way in which the existing partners can see themselves being repaid what they have put into the firm. If one of them is nearing retirement age and has put a high level of capital into the firm, he will want to take this out when he retires; there may not be enough working capital to provide this; borrowing may be too expensive and the profits may not be sufficient to fund an annuity. The capital of the incoming partner may be seen as one way of providing this finance. This is likely to be the case where the partnership is over-capitalised, where capital profits are repayable, and where goodwill is an asset of the firm.

There are various ways in which the new partner can introduce capital. He could introduce it as a lump sum which will be immediately credited to his capital account, and he will, as with all capital contributions, have a right to its return when he retires. This presupposes that he has the lump sum already available which is not often the case. Even if he has the lump sum it may not be the ideal solution. Even if the firm pays him some interest on capital, he only has the right to take the equivalent amount out when he retires, and bearing in mind inflation, this is not an attractive investment.

If the firm requires the introduction of a lump sum which he does not have, then the new partner can borrow to raise the amount. From the firm's point of view, either of the two ways of producing capital so far mentioned is attractive because the capital sum is available instantly (eg to fund the expansion) and not by instalments. It may also mean that existing partners can withdraw some capital from the firm, thus preventing it from becoming over capitalised. From the new partner's point of view a loan means that he pays for his capital contribution over a period of years. The interest repayments on the borrowing qualify for tax relief as a loan to purchase a share in a business (Finance Act 1974, Sched 1). However, the lender may require the new partner to provide some security for the loan which he may not have, particularly if his home is already heavily mortgaged. A fundamental problem may be that his income just is not high enough to fund the repayments on the loan.

Another possibility is that he is required to leave a certain amount of undrawn profit in the firm each year, thus gradually introducing capital. It is a very common way of financing working capital requirements in many firms.

There are no hard-and-fast rules on how the new partner can best provide capital. The eventual agreement will depend as we have seen on the new partner's individual circumstances, on the capital structure of the firm and on its future capital requirements.

If the new partner is worried about the capital structure of the firm (particularly if goodwill features large in the accounts thus requiring incoming partners to provide large sums to pay for their share), it could be the time to decide that goodwill should be abolished. This will avoid the continuing problem of how to pay retiring partners for their share of the goodwill. If goodwill is to be abolished and taken out of the accounts then some compensation will have to be given to the existing partners not only because this is just, but also because there might otherwise be a charge to CTT. Thus there must be some bona fide commercial bargain. Compensation could be provided by giving the existing partners an increased share in the profits or by topping up their retirement annuity schemes so that on retirement they receive not the payment for goodwill, but a larger pension.

The new partner should also enquire whether interest is to be paid on his capital, remembering that this can only be done by agreement and also that this interest will nevertheless be taxed as earned profit.

(*c*) *Steps to be taken on the introduction of a new partner*

The partnership agreement will have to be amended. A completely new deed could be drawn up which deals with the new and existing partners; this might be the case either where there was no deed before or where the old deed is now out of date. The existing deed or agreement should be looked at and the new partner can propose appropriate amendments. Alternatively, it may not be necessary to draw up a completely new deed; the terms agreed between the incoming partner and the existing partners can be negotiated and incorporated in an agreement which will then be read in conjunction with the original agreement. Bearing in mind the likely inequality of bargaining power, it would be sensible for the incoming partner to seek advice both from accountants and also from a solicitor either on an informal basis or if necessary by instructing that solicitor professionally.

The firm will have to consider whether to elect for continuance for tax purposes, and if they do so decide it will be necessary to sign the election.

2 The tax effects of a change in partners

(*a*) *Income tax*

When a new equity partner enters the partnership, or when one leaves the partnership, the firm is treated as having been discontinued, and a new firm started. This is not the effect of the introduction of a salaried partner.

Section 154(1) of the Income and Corporation Taxes Act 1970 provides that the business is automatically treated as having ceased and a new business started at the date of the change. This is so, for tax purposes, whatever the articles may say as between the partners themselves. The result of s 154(1) is that prima facie the opening and closing years rules apply when there is a change of partners (see ss 116 to 118 and p 35). Thus in the actual year of the deemed cessation of the business and in its penultimate and antepenultimate years if the Revenue so elect, the firm will be taxed on actual profits made rather than on a preceding year basis. In the three years after the change, the profits made in the first year will wholly or partly form the basis of assessment. However, s 154(2) allows the partners to elect that the firm shall be treated as continuing so that the normal preceding year basis of assessment will continue to apply. This election can only be made if certain conditions are fulfilled. First, there must be at least one partner common to both the old and the new firms; secondly, all partners (or their executors) before and after the change must jointly make the election by notice to the inspector within two years of the change. The election may be revoked provided the notice of revocation is signed by all interested parties and made within the limit of two years from the date of the change.

Thus, both incoming and outgoing partners should agree to sign the election should it be required of them and a clause to this effect will be incorporated in the partnership deed. As this might have the effect of the new partner paying more tax than he would otherwise have to (see p 119) there should also be a clause whereby the other partners agree to indemnify him against any increased liability to income tax as a result of the election. The decision as to whether or not to elect for continuance is one which needs careful and detailed consideration and one which can only be made in conjunction with the firm's accountants. As well as having an effect on the amount of tax the partners will pay, it will also have an effect on other aspects of the firm's tax and accounting.

As a general rule, where profits are rising then it is advantageous to elect for continuance as *Example 1* shows. When profits are decreasing then the election should not be made unless the tax saving is outweighed by the inconvenience. However, the tax saving on a cessation and recommencement may be such that it is worth not making the election thus providing the firm with more working capital at the expense of the Inland Revenue.

Example 1:
A and *B* in partnership make up their accounts to 31 December each year. The following profits are made: 1979—£20,000; 1980—£24,000; 1981—£30,000; 1982—£32,000. On 1 January 1983 they decide to admit *C* as a partner. Profits in 1983 amount to £36,000. Should they elect under s 154(2) of ICTA 1970?

Non election (partnership is dissolved 31 December 1982).

	£
Tax year 1982–83 (3/4 × 32,000 + 1/4 × 36,000)	33,000
Tax year 1981–82 (PYB: 24,000) Actual basis: 1/4 × 32,000 + 3/4 × 30,000 =	30,500
Tax year 1980–81 (PYB: 20,000) Actual basis: 1/4 × 30,000 + 3/4 × 24,000	25,500
Tax payable on this sum	89,000

(Since the actual basis will produce higher tax than allowing the partnership to be taxed on the preceding year basis in the penultimate and ante-penultimate years the Revenue will exercise their election under s 118.)

Election

Tax year 1982–83 (PYB)	30,000
Tax year 1981–82 (PYB)	24,000
Tax year 1980–81 (PYB)	20,000
Tax payable on this sum	74,000

Therefore elect

Example 2:
A and *B* in partnership make up their accounts to 31 December each year. The following profits are made: 1979—£40,000; 1980—£38,000; 1981—£32,000; 1982—£30,000. On 1 January 1983 they admit *C* as a partner. Profits in 1983 amount to £28,000. Should they elect under s 154(2) of the ICTA 1970?

Non election (partnership dissolved 31 December 1982)

	£
Tax year 1982–83 (3/4 × 30,000 × 1/4 × 28,000)	29,500
Tax year 1981–82 PYB (Actual basis: 1/4 × 30,000 + 3/4 × 32,000 = 31,500)	38,000
Tax year 1980–81 PYB (Actual basis: 1/4 × 32,000 + 3/4 × 38,000 = 36,500)	40,000
Tax payable on this sum	107,500

(Since the PYB will produce higher tax than the actual basis in the tax year 1981–82 and 1980–81, the Revenue will not exercise their election for actual basis.)

Election

	£
Tax year 1982–83 (PYB)	32,000
Tax year 1981–82 (PYB)	38,000
Tax year 1980–81 (PYB)	40,000
Tax payable on this sum	110,000

Therefore do not elect

In a professional firm, it is to be hoped that profits are rising and thus the election should be made.

Other problems occur if the election is not made. If the firm is being assessed to tax on the cash basis of accounting and the cessation provisions apply, the Revenue will require a switch to the earnings basis for the first three years at least of the 'new firm'. The firm will have to switch from one basis of accounting to another, with the possibility of then having to switch back again after three years. If this is so then the work in progress and debtors which were not assessed to tax in the old firm because of the cash basis will have to be brought in as post cessation receipts. In addition capital allowances will have to be recalculated and if tax relief is being claimed on a capital sum for a pension over a number of years, this will have to be adjusted.

(*b*) *Capital gains tax*

When a partner enters the firm and takes a share in the profits of the firm, then unless otherwise agreed (and it is unlikely to be), he takes a share in the asset surpluses in the same ratio as he takes a share in the profits. As has already been discussed (see p 126) provided there is no upward revaluation of the assets, and provided there is no cash paid between the partners, then the partners who dispose of a part of their share in the asset surpluses will bear no liability to CGT. As also explained the Revenue are unlikely to substitute market value as the consideration because it will be shown that the existing partners have no intention to make a gift to the new partner; there is a bona fide commercial transaction providing consideration. The existing partners dispose of a share in their asset surpluses and the incoming partner covenants to devote the whole of his time to the partnership and to work diligently, etc. As we have seen *Att-Gen* v *Boden* decided (in relation to estate duty) that mutual covenants in a partnership deed amounted to full consideration for the purchase of goodwill.

If the incoming partner does provide cash on his entry into the firm, then it should be understood that if this is his capital contribution and is credited to his capital account, no cash has been paid between the partners and so there is no assessment to CGT. However if on entry he brings in any money that is not credited to his capital account, but rather is credited to the existing partners' capital accounts then there can be an assessment to CGT. Even if a cash payment is made outside the accounts, in the form of a premium to the partners as individuals to compensate them for an increase in the value of assets or goodwill which does not show up in the firm's accounts, nevertheless there may be an assessment to CGT.

This assessment need not necessarily lead to a liability to CGT bearing in mind the £5,000 exemption and also the reliefs on retirement.

(*c*) *Capital transfer tax*

The incoming partner may in the partnership deed agree that on his retirement goodwill will automatically accrue to the remaining partners without payment to him; he may by the agreement give the remaining partners an option to purchase his share in the partnership assets at an undervalue. In both these cases, his share immediately on entering the partnership is less than it might otherwise have been and therefore as he has received nothing for this gift to the other partners, prima facie there is CTT liability. There has been a disposition as a result of which the value of his estate immediately after the disposition is less than it would have been. However, as explained before, provided the arrangements fall within s 20(4) of the Finance Act 1975 so that the transaction is one at arm's length without gratuitous intent, CTT will be avoided. Section 20(4) is complied with by the mutual covenants in the deed, to work full time in the business and to provide reciprocal pension arrangements.

If, unhappily, CTT were to be relevant, it is unlikely at this early stage in his life that the incoming partner would have to pay any tax, bearing in mind the fact that the first £55,000 is taxed at a nil rate and any gift made now will fall out of cumulation in ten years' time.

3 Branch offices

Expanding the firm may make it necessary to look for further office accommodation. If this is so, one possibility is to open an office in a nearby town so as to extend the catchment area. What implications are there in setting up such a branch office? The first point to note is that providing the office is merely a branch of the principal office, there is no need to register the branch office separately for VAT purposes, nor would the local tax office (if different from the tax office of the principal office) have to be notified, since it is assumed that all the PAYE returns would be made from the cashier's office in the principal office.

A firm of solicitors who wish to open a branch office must bear in mind the provisions of the Solicitors' Practice Rules 1975. These rules were drawn up in order to ensure proper management and supervision of a solicitors' office at times when it is open to the public. The minimum standard of supervision as laid down by these Rules is that every office, during all hours that it is open to the public, must be *managed* by either a solicitor holding a current practising certificate, or by a Fellow of the Institute of Legal Executives who has been admitted as such for not less than five years. In this context, management means that such solicitor, or suitably qualified legal executive, must normally be in attendance at the office during those hours when the office is open to the public. The Rules, however, acknowledge the fact that employees and principals alike are entitled to take holidays and that such persons managing the office will need to be absent on certain occasions on clients' affairs. In addition to the duty imposed on partners to ensure proper management, there is a further duty imposed concerned with overall supervision. The Rules require that every office on each day that it is open to the public must be attended by a solicitor who holds a current practising certificate, and who has been admitted as a solicitor for at least three years. It is up to this suitably qualified solicitor to spend sufficient time at the office in order to ensure adequate control of the staff employed there, and also to make available proper facilities for the clients of the firm to consult with him as needs be.

It follows that a solicitor who has been admitted as such for at least three years can carry out both the management and supervision of the office, but if the management is to be in the hands of a solicitor with less than three years' qualification, further steps need to be taken in order to comply with the Rules. It should also be noted that both parts of the Rules apply only where the office is open to the public. One way of lessening the impact of these Rules is therefore to open the branch office to the public on only say two days per week. In order to comply with the supervision requirements, a solicitor only needs to have been admitted for the three-year period; he does not need to have had three practising certificates, nor need he have worked in private practice for this period of time.

As a result of these Rules, a solicitor who has been qualified for less than three years is not permitted to run a branch office without supervision. He may not establish himself as a sole practitioner nor may he practise in partnership alone with someone of like seniority. The Rules do not, however, prevent a solicitor with less than three years' qualification from entering into partnership, so long as at least one partner has the necessary qualification to discharge the duty of daily attendance under the Rules.

Chapter 10

Leaving the Firm

1 Reasons for leaving

(a) Death or bankruptcy

The death of a partner automatically dissolves the partnership unless the partners have agreed otherwise (Partnership Act, s 33: see p 50). The partnership thus becomes at risk not only from the partners themselves but also from the personal representatives of the deceased who may have no particular attachment to the firm or its continuation. To avoid the complete dissolution of the firm on death, the articles should provide that death of a partner dissolves the firm only in so far as that partner is concerned. The effect of this is that the remaining partners cannot, because of the death, seize the opportunity to take themselves and their money out of the firm. The personal representatives of the deceased partners retain a right to the deceased's share of the partnership assets for the benefit of the estate and if the articles are silent as to how this is to be paid, then they have a right to insist that his share be paid immediately, enforceable through the courts (see ss 39 and 44: p 52). The wise firm will therefore include in the articles a clause as to how the deceased's partner's share is to be paid and whether, eg, the firm is to pay an annuity to his widow or dependants. If the firm is being wound up as a result of the death then although the remaining partners have continuing authority to do that which is necessary to wind up the firm (see s 38) the personal representatives do not. However, if any land forms part of the firm's assets then this is vested in them and their consent is needed as to its disposal.

Section 33 also provides that bankruptcy dissolves the firm unless the articles otherwise provide. The same considerations apply as discussed above except that the bankrupt partner has no authority in the winding-up. In this case, however, the partner is still alive but will no longer be a partner.

(*b*) *Voluntary retirement on grounds of age*

Retirement of itself does not bring the partnership to an end. The only way a partner can retire is to leave within the terms of the articles or if necessary dissolve the firm. In this context we are considering a partner who is leaving the firm because he has decided he is too old to carry on. The articles may provide that a partner can retire on giving six months' notice—in this case again it is sensible to provide that this notice dissolves the firm only in so far as the retiring partner is concerned. The articles might provide that a partner must retire on reaching a certain age. If the articles are silent then retirement will have to be arranged by negotiation as it would seem pointless to have to force a complete dissolution of the firm with all its consequences.

Again the wise firm will have in its articles several clauses dealing with the financial position of the retiring partner. The type and effect of these clauses is discussed on pp 87–94.

(*c*) *Early dissatisfaction*

A partner may wish to leave the firm before retiring age, eg because he has fallen out with the other partners, he wants to join another firm or set up his own firm. If the articles are silent as to whether he can do this, then it is a partnership at will, and he can leave merely by giving notice to the other partners. The whole firm is then dissolved and he has a right to his share in the assets and any profits owing to him, and any asset surpluses which he enforces through ss 39 and 44 of the Act. This will obviously be unsatisfactory for the remaining partners and could be disastrous. Thus they will do all they can in this situation to negotiate a settlement with the partner who is leaving. If the articles provide that a partner can only leave on giving six months' notice then at least this gives the firm some time to consider its position; if this is supported with a clause as to how a partner is to be paid his share in this situation then many of the difficulties of the remaining partners may be overcome, although the outgoing partner might want to negotiate more advantageous repayment terms if he is to join another firm, or set up on his own and needs capital with which to do so. If the articles provide for a fixed term partnership or that, eg, a partner can only leave at a certain age or for reasons of ill health, then the only way that a partner can leave early, other than by agreement, is to go to the court and seek an order of the court that the partnership should be dissolved under s 35 (see p 51). The partner who merely wishes to leave to further his own career is unlikely to get such an order; the partner who wishes to leave because the firm has run into major problems may be successful.

(*d*) *Expulsion*

If a partner breaks the terms of the agreement or otherwise acts in a way detrimental to the partnership, the remaining partners will have to decide whether they wish to be rid of him and if so how. In the last resort it may be necessary to ask the court for a dissolution; alternatively the partnership may be dissolved by giving the required period of notice—but the remaining partners are likely to want the defaulting partner's removal without having to dissolve the firm entirely.

Section 25 provides that it is only possible to expel a partner by majority vote if the articles so provide, otherwise unanimous consent is needed. In the nature of things this is not likely to be forthcoming and so it is advisable to have a clause dealing with expulsion (see p 95).

Expelled partners, like any others who leave the firm, will want to take their share of the assets and profits and have a right to do so except in the unlikely event that the expulsion clause denies them this right. Thus the clause should deal with how the expelled partner is to be paid his share—very often the same clause will apply to death, retirement and expulsion.

2 Steps to be taken on leaving

(*a*) *To avoid continuing liability*

On pp 18–21 we discussed the effect of ss 14, 17(2) and 36 of the Act in detail. Briefly as a reminder, section 17(2) provides that a partner who retires from (in the sense of leaves) the firm does not thereby cease to be liable for partnership debts and obligations incurred before his retirement. Thus he is fully liable in contract and tort for anything that happened before he left the firm. His creditors, or those injured by his or the firm's tort, will be able to sue him, whatever the articles may say. However, it is usual to include in the partnership deed a clause that the remaining partners will indemnify the outgoing partner for any liabilities incurred before he leaves. Thus although he might be sued by a third party he can recover anything he has to pay from the remaining partners. The remaining partners would do well therefore to ensure that before a partner leaves there is no large outstanding liability. Where tort is concerned, the professional indemnity policy will cover this situation, except, eg, where the articled clerk in the course of his employment has driven (rather than advised) negligently. The only way to avoid the continuing contractual liability to third parties is by a contract of novation (see pp 18–19)—either an express contract or one inferred from a course of dealings. If the third party has enforced an obligation against only the existing partners in the past, he cannot now seek to pursue the retired partner.

The retired partner is also at risk because unless he gives the required notices under s 36, he will find that he is knowingly suffering himself to be held out as a partner under s 14 and thus liable for any contractual debt incurred in reliance on such a representation. The steps that he must ensure are taken are as follows:

1 Actual notice of his retirement must be given to existing clients or suppliers. This can take the form of a letter or circular to existing clients. It is not in breach of the Solicitors' Practice Rules (providing that it does not amount to touting) and therefore can serve as a reminder that the firm still exists. However, it is probably sufficient for the purposes of s 36 that the next time the firm communicates with a client or supplier, the letter heads are up to date.
2 Notice must be inserted in the *London Gazette* to comply with s 36(2).
3 The letter heads must be changed—either new letter heads will be necessary or the retired partner should ensure that his name is crossed out or, if relevant, the word consultant appears next to it. As he is only liable if he holds himself out or knowingly allows others to do so, it is not necessary for him laboriously to cross out his name on each sheet of paper; the agreement of the remaining partners that this will be done will be sufficient to avoid s 14.

(*b*) *Income tax election*

As previously explained (pp 141–144) any change in the membership of the firm is treated for income tax purposes as a cessation of that firm (s 154(1) of the Income and Corporation

Taxes Act 1970). The retirement of a partner, or his death or expulsion, will amount to such a change. To avoid the effects of s 154(1) the deed will contain a clause whereby a partner who is leaving agrees to the signing of the income tax election under s 154(2) should this be required by the remaining partners. They in turn agree to indemnify the retiring partner against any increase in tax. This agreement will bind personal representatives of a deceased partner. Thus, on leaving, it is advisable for the partner to sign the election there and then for future use by the remaining partners if it is to the advantage of the firm.

(*c*) *Other steps*

All deeds, drafts, letters and documents relating to the firm should remain with the firm or be delivered to the firm.

3 The financial position of the partner who is leaving

The partner who is leaving will have a right to any undrawn profits and interest on capital owing to him; he will also have a right to withdraw his capital. He has a statutory right to any asset surpluses under s 44 of the Partnership Act if the firm is dissolved, but whether in fact he has this right will usually depend on the relevant clause in the articles. He has no right to any income from the partnership after his retirement unless this has been agreed, eg in the form of an annuity from the firm or a consultancy fee or unless s 42 of the Partnership Act applies (see p 78). Of course his income requirements may be met by the payments he has been making over the years into a retirement annuity scheme to provide a pension. Many of the payments to be received by the outgoing partner will have tax consequences either for the firm or the partner himself. While discussing the various possible ways of providing for payment to the retired partner, the tax effects will also be considered.

(*a*) *Profits, etc*

At the date when a partner leaves the firm there is likely to be owing to him an amount of undrawn profit to which he is entitled and possibly interest on capital. He has a right to be paid this whether or not the articles so specify. If, however, there is a clause dealing with provision for the outgoing partner it is probable that there will be included a statement setting a time limit on payment for the same. It will be necessary to take an account from the date of the last previous account until the date of leaving in order to ascertain the amount of profit owing. This profit and interest on capital if any will be taxed in the normal way.

(*b*) *Capital*

A partner has a right to be repaid his capital—this means that he will be paid the amount of his original capital contribution and any further capital contribution he has made over the years. Unless this is repaid to him in the form of an annuity which then counts as income from his point of view and so is subject to income tax, the repayment of capital has no tax effects. He merely receives back what he put into the firm which was credited to his capital account. There has been no disposal for CGT and in any event no gain has been made on this capital. If the reason for the partner leaving is his death, then of course his capital forms part of his estate for CTT purposes.

The remaining partners have to find the money with which to make the capital repayment. If this is substantial, and in many firms the senior partner has built up considerable sums of capital over the years if only by leaving undrawn profits in the firm, the remaining partners have to find some means of paying it. If the articles are silent on this matter, then they should pay it straight away. If they do not, s 42 of the Act provides that either interest is payable at 5%, or the retired partner is to receive such share of the profits as the court finds attributable to his share, until such time as it is paid back. The articles can be drawn so that this repayment of capital is not such a burden on the remaining partners. There are various ways of doing this as we have seen.

Instalment payments. A suggested way of drafting the clause might be that a certain sum was to be payable in the near future, with the balance to be paid by instalments together with interest (to compensate the outgoing partner for being kept out of his money); provision should also be made in the event of non-payment. Thus, let us say that the partner's capital account shows that £20,000 is due to him; the clause might read as follows:

The amount of capital at the date of his ceasing to be a partner shall be paid as to £5,000 within six months of his ceasing to be a partner and thereafter by four equal annual instalments together with 10% interest per annum on the unpaid instalments from the date of the partner ceasing to be a partner, the first instalment to be paid one year after the said date. In the event of any payment, annual instalment or interest or any part thereof being in arrear and unpaid for thirty days the whole balance shall forthwith become payable and shall carry interest at 10% per annum until paid.

For the outgoing partner, this £5,000 might not be a sufficient lump sum for his plans on retirement and so a larger figure might be negotiated, preferably on his entry to the firm.

Payment as soon as practicable. Another possibility might be that his capital should be paid in entirety 'as soon as practicable' after he leaves the firm. This clause would cause difficulties for a firm where one or several of the partners had built up very large capital contributions, as the remaining partners might find that they had to borrow heavily to repay the capital.

Life assurance. One of the ways of providing for the repayment of capital is by the partners entering into reciprocal arrangements in the partnership agreement as to insurance. This enables an outgoing partner to be compensated for his share, or his dependants to be paid in the case of his dying before retirement. Each partner might agree to take out an endowment policy on his own life for his own benefit. Tax relief is claimable on the premiums. The sum he receives on maturity of the policy will be free of CGT. This sum will constitute the repayment of his capital share under the partnership agreement. If he dies early, the lump sum payable on death will be his capital repayment and form part of his estate. It may be liable to CTT. Another possibility is that each partner insures his own life but this is written in trust so that the other partners benefit. From the policy moneys payable on early death or retirement to the continuing partners the partner or his dependants can be paid his capital share. This arrangement avoids CGT liability and in most cases will not attract CTT.

(*c*) *Share in the assets*

We have discussed the assets of a firm and the fact that each partner has a right to a share in the asset surpluses in the same ratio as he shares profits. By asset surpluses is meant that which is left after all debts have been paid, and the partners have been paid their capital. Such assets are likely to include premises, equipment and possibly goodwill. The first problem is whether the outgoing partner should be paid for his share in the assets and if so how and at what valuation. The second problem is one of tax—put briefly if he is paid the full market value of the assets he is likely to have made a gain which will be liable to CGT; if he is not paid in full value he is making a gift to the remaining partners which may attract CTT. Let us look at the possibilities.

Payment at full market value. The articles will provide that an account shall be taken, in the usual way, from the date of the last account until the day the outgoing partner ceases to be a partner and the assets of the firm shall be valued for the purposes of taking the account. The clause will then continue by providing how this is to be paid to the outgoing partner, ie whether in one lump sum, or by instalments. Usually the same approach will be applied to both capital repayment and payment for his share in the assets. The outgoing partner has, by giving up his share in the profits and asset surpluses of the firm to the remaining partners, made a disposal of a chargeable asset for the purposes of CGT. By looking at the valuation of the assets when he entered the firm or what he paid when he entered the firm and the then asset surplus sharing ratios the acquisition cost can be ascertained and set against the present valuation to establish the level of gain. However, although the potential liability to CGT may be high there are certain reliefs which may be available. First, the first £5,000 of gain is exempt from CGT. Secondly, retirement relief may apply. If the outgoing partner is sixty-five or over, and has been a partner in the firm for ten years or more then he can claim relief on a gain of £50,000. If he is sixty or over and has been in the firm for less than ten years he can nevertheless claim relief but at a lower level (see p 43). Retirement relief applies to assets belonging to the firm but a Revenue Practice Statement of 4 January 1973 extended the relief to assets belonging to a partner and not the firm, but which are used for the partnership business. Relief is restricted if a rent has been charged. Thus a partner who owns premises which have been used by the firm and on retirement sells the premises to the firm will be able to claim full relief subject to age, etc, unless he has been charging the firm rent for the use of the premises, in which case the relief he can claim will be less.

Payment at less than market value. This approach particularly applies to goodwill although it might apply to all the assets of the firm. Thus for example it is usual to find in a deed a clause by which the share of the outgoing partner in the goodwill of the business accrues to the continuing partners without the outgoing partner being entitled to any payment. Or it may be provided in the articles that in valuing the assets of the firm for the purpose of ascertaining the partner's share, book valuation shall be used. If the assets have not been revalued for some considerable time then the partner is disposing of his share in them at an undervalue. In each case he has given something back to the remaining partners without receiving any or full consideration for it. In either case, CGT is only going to be payable if the retiring partner has actually made a gain and this may be covered by retirement relief. This is unless the Revenue substitute market value, which they will not do if they are satisfied that there has been a bona fide commercial transaction. Because the retiring partner by accepting no payment or a lower payment for returning his share of the assets to the remaining partners has therefore suffered a diminution in value of his estate he is prima facie liable to CTT. As we have already seen, provided it can be argued that this is part of a bona fide commercial transaction made at arm's length without gratuitous intent under s 20(4) of the Finance Act 1975 then CTT will not be payable. The mutual covenants in the deed as to work and pension arrangements should provide the consideration required (*Att-Gen* v *Boden*). A partner who agrees to either of these possibilities makes a disposition for CTT purposes when he signs the agreement and a further disposition when he retires and carries out the terms of the agreement. If CTT is to be payable, it can be assessed on both occasions, credit being given for the earlier calculation.

Annuities. Rather than pay a lump sum to the outgoing partner for his share in the firm's assets, the partners may agree that in return for the outgoing partner's share accruing to the remaining partners, the firm will pay an annuity to the retired partner or to the dependants of a deceased partner. As well as compensating the retired partner for his share, it provides much needed income for him in his retirement. In addition there may be CGT advantages and income tax relief for the firm, who do not of course have to find such large sums with which to pay him back. The payments for the former partner's share are thus spread over a long period, and for the retired partner it may provide additional income to that from his retirement annuity scheme. The payment of the annuity does depend on the continuation of the firm and thus it may not be a satisfactory arrangement where the firm is small and perhaps not long established. For the small firm, too, the annuity might be a heavy financial burden. The clause in the partnership deed will specify the length of time during which the annuity will be paid, eg ten years, the amount of the annual payments, eg calculated by reference to a percentage of the firm's profits each year, and whether and if so to what extent an annuity will be paid to the retired partner's spouse and dependants in the event of his death.

We have seen that if the retired partner receives a lump sum for his share then, subject to any appropriate relief, eg retirement relief, he will be liable to capital gains tax. An advantage of payment by way of annuity is that provided the annuity falls within certain limits it will not attract CGT even though it is in reality payment for his share.

The general rule is that the Revenue will treat the capitalised value of the annuity as consideration received for the disposal of his partnership share and thus assess him to CGT on any gain made (CGTA 1979, s 31(3)). However, if the annuity falls within certain limits laid down in the Revenue Practice Statement of 17 January 1975, as amended by a Press Release of 12 January 1979 (see Appendix 2) then the Revenue will not apply a capitalised value to it thereby ensuring that it does not attract CGT.

The practice statements lay down the following rules. The annuity will not be capitalised unless 'it is more than can be regarded as reasonable recognition of the past contribution of work and effort by the partner to the partnership'. The statement then goes on to define what is meant by 'reasonable recognition' by reference to a formula. If the retired partner was a partner in the firm for ten years or more then an annuity not exceeding two-thirds of his average share of profits in the best three of his last seven years as a full time partner will be treated as reasonable (para 8—see Appendix 2). It was the case that if in addition to an annuity a lump sum was paid, then the concession in the practice statement did not apply. However, by a further concession in the Press Release of 12 January 1979, a combination of a lump sum and an annuity in return for the accrual of the retired partner's share will not attract CGT if the aggregate of the annuity plus one-ninth of the lump sum does not fall outside the formula in para 8 above. The effect of this is that the capitalised value of the annuity will not be treated as consideration but the lump sum will nevertheless be so treated. However, if the lump sum falls within the limit of retirement relief then no CGT will be payable, or alternatively the lump sum can be at such a level that no gain or one not exceeding £5,000 is made.

The firm that pays the annuity will be able to claim income tax relief. The annuity is an annual payment within ss 52 and 53 of the Income and Corporation Taxes Act 1970 (see p 29). Thus the firm must deduct income tax at basic rate before making payment to the retired partner or his dependants. The annuity is deductible in computing the total income of the paying partners and as it falls within s 457 of the Income and Corporation Taxes Act 1970 it will give tax relief not only as far as basic rate tax is concerned but also where excess liability is concerned. To fall within s 457 it has to be paid under a liability incurred for full consideration and must be payable either under the terms of a partnership agreement or in connection with the acquisition of a share in the business by the paying partner. The paying partners of the firm are acquiring the retired partner's share in the assets of the firm for full consideration and thus can claim relief under s 457.

If the annuity continues after the partner's death for his spouse and/or dependants, then this may create income tax problems as s 457(4) provides that full tax relief will not be available if the annuity is to be paid after the death of the partner and more than ten years after he left the firm. This is why it is usual to provide in the partnership agreement that the annuity should only be payable for ten years.

In the recipient partner's hands the income is prima facie investment income which means it is subject not only to basic and higher rate tax but also investment income surcharge. However, by s 16 of the Finance Act 1974 it can be treated as earned income thus avoiding the surcharge if certain conditions are fulfilled. Section 16 applies where the annuity is paid under the partnership agreement or some agreement replacing it to the retired partner, his widow or dependants and where the reason for the partner leaving the firm is age, illness or death. If these conditions are fulfilled then the annuity will be treated as earned income up to a certain limit; the limit is 50% of the average of the former partner's share of the profits in the best three of the last seven years of assessment in which he was required to devote substantially the whole of his time to acting as a partner.

(*d*) *Income*

Annuity from the firm. This provides income for the retired partner or his dependants for at least ten years as discussed above.

Pension under a retirement annuity scheme. As discussed earlier, a self-employed person should make provision for his own pension (see p 91) and indeed this may be written into the partnership agreement as a requirement (p 197). Provided the scheme falls within the conditions of s 226 of the Income and Corporation Taxes Act then tax relief is available on the premiums that the partner pays during his working life. The receipt of the pension is treated as earned income as long as the premiums qualified for tax relief. In addition the pension may be partially commuted for a tax free lump sum.

Consultancy fees. On retirement the retired partner might wish to continue to do some work and the firm might benefit from his continued association with it, particularly if his reputation was high amongst clients. A consultancy arrangement can be entered into. A consultant is not a partner. The consultant will be paid a fee perhaps for the next five years after retirement. If this is no more than a different way of paying him for his share in the partnership assets, ie it is linked with the transfer of his share, then the fee is taxed in the retired partner's hands as investment income (*Hale* v *Shea* [1965] 1 WLR 290). If there is a genuine consultancy, ie the consultant actually does work for the firm, then the fees will be earned income in his hands and will be deductible expenditure in computing the firm's profits (*Copeman* v *Flood* [1941] 1 KB 202). It also means that any income which is outside the limits of s 16 of the Finance Act 1974 can still be earned income if the fees are reasonable for the amount of work done by the consultant.

Part III

Traders' Choice of Business Medium

Chapter 11

Choice of Business Medium

1 Introduction

In a professional relationship it is often impossible, where two or more practise together, to practise otherwise than as partners. For example, solicitors are forbidden by s 24 of the Solicitors Act 1974 from practising in a corporate form. If, however, the nature of the business is trade, then serious consideration must be given to the best medium in which to trade. Assuming that there are two or more persons who wish to trade together, their choice of business medium is basically to trade as a partnership, or to form a company and to trade through this medium. The major points of difference between these two types of trading medium are listed below.

2 Creation

(a) Partnership

No particular formalities need be complied with in order to form a partnership. Once the criteria in s 1 of the Partnership Act 1890 are satisfied a partnership is in existence. However, in practice it is wise to have a formal agreement drawn up embodying the terms of the partnership; in the absence of such an agreement, the Partnership Act will imply certain terms, rules and regulations. Consequently, the cost of forming a partnership (as opposed to capitalising a partnership) can range from nothing to a large fee payable to solicitors who draft complex partnership articles.

As to numbers, unless the partnership is a professional one, the maximum number of partners who can trade together as such is twenty (s 434 of the Companies Act 1948).

(b) Company

A company has a far more rigid structure than a partnership, and consequently there are many more formalities to be complied with in respect of formation. A company which is limited by shares (the most common and convenient type of company for use as a trading medium) must be registered under the provisions of the Companies Acts 1948–81. These Acts require certain documents to be submitted to the Registrar of Companies together with a fee of £50 before registration. Once the company is registered, the Registrar will issue a certificate of registration. This procedure obviously takes time (anything between six and ten weeks), and until the certificate is issued, the company is not in being. Accordingly it is possible to purchase a 'shelf company', ie a company which has been formed with certain standard documents, no shares having been issued, and no trading commenced. The advantage of buying such a company is that the medium is available for immediate use, and can immediately enter into contracts; the disadvantage is that the documentation will be in a standard form, and may not necessarily be precisely what is required. If this is so steps must be taken to amend the documentation as necessary. Costs of a 'shelf company' vary according to the type purchased, but at the time of writing, the average cost is approximately £100. If it is intended to form a company from scratch, then in addition to the registration fee of £50 there will be further fees to pay in respect of the cost of drafting the necessary documentation. Whichever company is taken (ie whether a 'shelf company' or one formed from scratch), on the issue of shares, capital duty is payable at the rate of 1% of the consideration.

As to numbers, since the Companies Act 1980 there is no longer any restriction on the size of a company, whether the company is a private one or a public one.

3 Personality

(a) Partnership

A partnership has no legal personality of its own, but is merely the partners trading together under one name. The partners are consequently liable for all the debts and obligations incurred by and on behalf of the firm, and their ultimate risk must be individual bankruptcy. Although it is possible to sue the partners in the firm name (see p 15) this is not an indication of a separate personality, but merely a convenient method of suing the individual partners.

(b) Company

A company is in law a distinct and separate legal entity, and as such can sue, be sued, own property and be convicted in its own right of a criminal offence. It is therefore separate in all ways from its owners (the shareholders) and its managers (the directors). One consequence of this separate personality is that if the company is formed with limited liability, then apart from exceptional circumstances, the shareholders and directors will not be liable for the debts and obligations of the company. If the liability is limited by shares, then the shareholders are liable only up to the amount unpaid on their shares; if the shares are fully paid up (as is usual) then they cannot be held liable for any further sum. This concept of limited liability is obviously a major advantage of choosing the company as a means of trading. However, it must be remembered that despite the theoretical advantage, in practice there may well be restrictions on the extent to which the liability of members or directors of a company is limited. Many firms dealing with a newly formed company, and most banks lending to such a company, will insist on the contracts with the company being guaranteed by the shareholders and/or the directors. This means that two individuals faced with the choice of business medium may decide on a partnership, thus risking bankruptcy; or decide upon a company, and be forced to give personal guarantees, and yet again risk the possibility of bankruptcy. When dealing with ordinary members of the public who are unlikely to insist on such guarantees, the limited liability of a company does still have its advantages.

A further consequence of a company's own personality is its ability to give security by means of a floating charge. This is something that cannot be done by individuals or partners. Such a charge is an equitable charge on some or all of the assets of the company (both present and future), whereby the company is empowered to deal with those assets in the ordinary course of business. The floating nature of the charge remains as such until there is some default on behalf of the company and the necessary steps are taken to enforce the charge; at this point the charge is said to crystallise, and becomes a fixed charge on those assets over which it takes effect at the time of crystallisation. The ability to create such a charge is clearly an advantage that a company has over a partnership, since it makes the borrowing of money easier, by allowing the company to give security without affecting its right to deal with its assets. (The reason why a partnership cannot create such charges is that inasmuch as the charge is created over chattels, such as stock in trade, it would have to be registered under the Bills of Sale Acts 1878–82, and a detailed schedule of the assets charged must be set out in the charge form. This of itself means that the floating nature of such a charge would disappear. The Acts referred to expressly exclude their provisions as far as companies are concerned.)

4 Accounts and other publicity

(*a*) *Partnership*

An advantage that a partnership has over a company is the complete privacy of its accounts and financial arrangements. Such accounts as are prepared are for the partners themselves, and their professional advisers, and need not be made public in any way. Thus there is less chance of creditors of the partnership withdrawing credit facilities after the preparation of the accounts, if the accounts show that the firm is in financial difficulties. There was, until the Companies Act 1981 came into force, an obligation in certain circumstances to register under the Registration of Business Names Act 1916.

(*b*) *Company*

A company (whether public or private) must submit an Annual Return to the Registrar of Companies, which gives certain detailed information concerning the share capital, the shareholders, and the directors of the company. In addition under s 143 of the Companies Act 1948 certain resolutions passed by the company in general meeting must be sent to the Registrar within fifteen days. Since the Companies Act 1967, private companies as well as public companies must submit accounts to the Registrar of Companies, and these are consequently made public—anyone can inspect them by making the appropriate search at the Registry. These published accounts of a company gave limited information until the Companies Act 1981, which implemented the EEC fourth directive on Company Law, and which now requires detailed information to be revealed in the accounts (subject to certain exceptions for 'small' and 'medium sized' companies). There are penalties for failure to comply with these provisions as to the submission of accounts and other returns.

5 Flexibility

(a) Partnership

It should be obvious from what has been written in the earlier parts of this book that a major advantage of a partnership is its flexibility. No formalities are required to form the partnership; no returns need be made by the partners in respect of day to day decisions, and accounts; the partners take most decisions by majority and there is no split in the management power as in a company where the shareholders share certain powers with the directors. Further, although the Partnership Act 1890 does lay down a large number of regulations as regards this medium, many of these can be ignored in practice, since it is usually the intention of the partners which is paramount.

If the partners decide to branch out into something different, they can do so without formality. Subject to contrary intention being shown, s 24(8) of the Partnership Act 1890 provides that a change can be made in the nature of the partnership business with the consent of all the existing partners.

(b) Company

A company is a far more rigid medium than a partnership. Strict formalities have to be complied with in respect of formation, management, day to day running of the company, and indeed liquidation. Where this is perhaps shown best is in the doctrine of ultra vires which applies to a company and not to a partnership. When the company is formed it must include in a document called the memorandum of association a list of objects; ie the objects for which the company was formed. At common law if a company acted outside this list, then that transaction was not enforceable by either the company or the third party. If a company wishes to change its objects, then although this can be done in certain circumstances, these circumstances are limited, and the company must comply with the strict requirements of the Companies Acts. (There is now certain protection for the outsider dealing with a company which has acted ultra vires by virtue of s 9 of the European Communities Act 1972, but the extent of such protection has yet to be decided by the courts.)

6 Taxation

Many of the matters already discussed in this chapter are of importance in deciding in which medium to trade. However, most traders are interested in the answer to one question only when starting a business from scratch. That question is 'How much am I going to be able to take out of the business in the form of profit?' This in itself begs the obvious question of how much the taxman is going to take, and therefore how much will be left. For this reason, perhaps the most important consideration to be taken into account when deciding on the business medium is the taxation of profits.

(*a*) *Partnership*

When the business is starting from scratch, partnership has the great advantage in that profits are taxed under Schedule D, Case I or II, by applying the opening year rules under ss 116 and 117 of the Income and Corporation Taxes Act 1970; thereafter the normal preceding year basis of assessment applies (see p 35). The advantages of these provisions in relation to the deferred payment of tax have been dealt with in Parts I and II of this book. Further, because the partners are being taxed under Schedule D, Case I or II, the provisions of the taxing statutes relating to deductible expenditure are very much simpler than those provisions which apply to Schedule E. All trading or professional profits are taxed as income (up to a maximum rate of 60%) regardless of whether or not they have been withdrawn in the form of drawings.

All other matters being equal, it is arguable that the best medium in which to trade in the first few years of the business's life is that of a partnership, taking full advantage of the beneficial tax position. If the partnership makes losses for tax purposes in the first years of trading those losses can be set off against other profits as shown on p 34. In addition, as far as individuals are concerned (and this includes someone trading, or practising as a partner) they can take the benefit of s 30 of the Finance Act 1978 (see p 36).

Where the partners make capital gains and are thus liable to capital gains tax, each partner is entitled to his or her £5,000 annual exemption, and where the gain arises from dealings with partnership property, or property used by the partnership but belonging to the partners individually, then in the specified circumstances retirement relief under ss 124 and 125 of the Capital Gains Tax Act 1979 is available. Other reliefs such as replacement of business assets (ss 115–121), and gifts of assets (s 79 of the Finance Act 1980), might also be available.

Unless there is an intention to make a gift of a share in the partnership, or of the partnership property, capital transfer tax should cause no problems (see p 127). Where a gratuitous intent is shown, the relief for business property under Sched 10 to the Finance Act 1976 as amended will usually be available. The advantage of trading as a partnership is that in such circumstances, where the gift is of the business or an interest in a business, the amount of the relief is 50% without reference to any 'control' by the partner of the business.

Finally, where a partner wishes to borrow money from, say, a bank, to enable him to contribute capital to the partnership, such a loan will qualify for tax relief; ie the interest paid to the bank by the partner will be deductible for tax purposes in the hands of the partner (see s 75 of the Finance Act 1972 and Part III of Sched 1 to the Finance Act 1974).

(b) Company

Unlike a partnership, there are no separate opening year rules for companies; profits made by a company are liable to corporation tax, such profits being assessed on a current year basis. However, the type of company envisaged as being an alternative to a partnership is likely to have a small number of members (shareholders) all of whom are directors—the medium is likely to be of the nature of an 'incorporated partnership'. As such, the shareholder/directors are unlikely to leave any profit in the company which will be subjected to corporation tax; it is more likely that they will withdraw such profit by way of directors' fees. These fees, so long as they are reasonable (which in practice they will be) are deductible from the company's profits for corporation tax purposes, and if all the excess profits are taken as fees in this way, no corporation tax will be payable.

In the hands of the directors, the fees will be taxed as earned income under Schedule E. They will therefore be taxed on the current year basis, and the company should deduct the tax payable at source under the PAYE system. As mentioned before, any expenses incurred by the directors will not be so easily deductible for Schedule E purposes as they would for Schedule D, but if the company incurs the expense it may be deductible for corporation tax purposes.

In some circumstances, it may be thought necessary to take

profits out of the company in some other way than by directors' fees. This may be because profits are excessive, and the fees cannot be justified, or because an individual has invested in the company but is not a director. In these circumstances the choice is simple; either the profits are paid out to a shareholder by way of a dividend declared on the shares so held, or the investor is given a debenture by the company and receives his return by way of annual interest paid. Which is the most tax effective way? As far as the dividend is concerned, this payment is a qualifying distribution, and consequently on the payment the company must make an advance payment of corporation tax equal to three-sevenths (at the time of writing) of the payment to the shareholder. This means that to support a dividend of £7,000, the company must have at least £10,000 in cash. Secondly, the payment of the dividend merely amounts to a distribution of profit and is therefore not allowable as a deduction for corporation tax purposes. Where interest is paid on a debenture this will be deductible for corporation tax purposes in most circumstances, and provided it is not excessive, nor varies with profits, the payment will not be a qualifying distribution, and no advance corporation tax is payable. In the hands of the recipient both the dividend and the interest will be taxed as unearned income, and therefore if appropriate the investment income surcharge will apply.

If a company makes trading losses then these can be relieved against other profits, and one advantage that a company has over a partnership is that in certain circumstances trading losses can be used to relieve liability for capital gains. Although s 30 of the Finance Act 1978 (see p 36) does not apply to companies, there is some relief given by ss 52–67 of the Finance Act 1981.

Where a company makes a capital gain this gain is taxed as corporation tax, but in such a way that no matter what the rate of corporation tax that applies to the company, the capital gain will be taxed at an effective rate of 30%. The major disadvantage is that a company is not entitled to the £5,000 per year exemption, although it can apply for replacement of business asset relief (under ss 115–121 of the Capital Gains Tax Act 1979), if appropriate. If the gain is made by the shareholder disposing of his shares in his 'family company' and the shareholder is also a full-time director of the company, then, subject to the conditions of the relief, retirement relief under ss 124 and 125 of the Capital Gains Tax Act 1979 will be available. Further, if the shareholder disposes of his shares by way of a gift, then CTT becomes payable, but business property relief may be available. In these circumstances, much depends on whether the shareholder had 'control' of the company immediately before the transfer; if he did then the 50% relief is given. If he holds a minority interest only, then 20% relief is available.

Capital transfer tax should not cause a problem for the company itself since this is a tax on individuals. However, there are certain anti-avoidance provisions in the Finance Act 1975 which apply to 'close companies'; these provisions are beyond the scope of this book.

There are provisions in the Finance Acts 1972 and 1974 relating to loans to an individual in order to acquire ordinary share capital in a close company (ie broadly a company under the control of five or fewer persons), or to lend money to a close company. In the same way as for partnerships, any interest payable on these qualifying loans is eligible for tax relief.

Finally, it should be noted that in dealing with shares or securities in a company, an individual risks the possibility of being caught by the provisions of s 460 of the Income and Corporation Taxes Act 1970. These provisions are very complex but they are designed to catch the transactions which on the surface look like capital transactions (and thus if there is a gain would be liable to capital gains tax at the rate of 30% rather than income tax at a higher rate). Where it is shown that a tax advantage to the individual has occurred as a result of this transaction, then under s 460 the individual can, in specified circumstances, be charged to income tax on the profit (thus incurring very much higher tax rates) unless it can be shown that the transaction was a bona fide commercial one, and did not have as its main object the avoidance of tax.

7 Conclusion

In the first years of a business, it can be an advantage to commence as a partnership. This medium is an inexpensive one to form, and has the added advantage of not having too many formalities to comply with. The tax position of the partners is such as to defer much of the tax payable in the early years, thus making a healthy cash flow position for the firm. The profits are going to be taxed at a maximum rate of 60%, and after a period of time the business can be sold to a company which has been specifically formed for this purpose. This would be a particularly attractive course if the retained profits (ie undistributed profits) were large.

The rate of corporation tax extends from 40% to a maximum of 52%, clearly amounting to a tax saving if the trading were carried out through the medium of a company.

Also in the first years, much of the advantage of having limited liability will disappear if personal guarantees are sought by creditors. In later years if the business has built up considerable goodwill, and is transferred to a company, then limited liability will be an advantage: guarantees may no longer be required.

Care must also be taken in anticipating future problems relating to disposing of the business. In both business media, substantial saving in respect of capital taxes can be obtained, although generally if the disposal is by way of a gift, it is better to be a partner (for the purposes of business property relief for CTT) unless that person is a shareholder who also has 'control' of the company.

Appendix 1

Partnership Act 1890
(as amended)

An Act to declare and amend the Law of Partnership. [14th August 1890.]

Nature of Partnership

1 Definition of partnership

(1) Partnership is the relation which subsists between persons carrying on a business in common with a view of profit.

(2) But the relation between members of any company or association which is—

(*a*) Registered as a company under the Companies Act, 1862, or any other Act of Parliament for the time being in force and relating to the registration of joint stock companies; or

(*b*) Formed or incorporated by or in pursuance of any other Act of Parliament or letters patent, or Royal Charter; or

(*c*) A company engaged in working mines within and subject to the jurisdiction of the Stannaries:

is not a partnership within the meaning of this Act.

2 Rules for determining existence of partnership

In determining whether a partnership does or does not exist, regard shall be had to the following rules:

(1) Joint tenancy, tenancy in common, joint property, common property, or part ownership does not of itself create a partnership as to anything so held or owned, whether the tenants or owners do or do not share any profits made by the use thereof.

(2) The sharing of gross returns does not of itself create a partnership, whether the persons sharing such returns have or have not a joint or common right or interest in any property from which or from the use of which the returns are derived.

(3) The receipt by a person of a share of the profits of a business is prima facie evidence that he is a partner in the business, but the receipt of such a share, or of a payment contingent on or varying

with the profits of a business, does not of itself make him a partner in the business; and in particular—

(*a*) The receipt by a person of a debt or other liquidated amount by instalments, or otherwise out of the accruing profits of a business does not of itself make him a partner in the business or liable as such:

(*b*) A contract for the remuneration of a servant or agent of a person engaged in a business by a share of the profits of the business does not of itself make the servant or agent a partner in the business or liable as such:

(*c*) A person being the widow or child of a deceased partner, and receiving by way of annuity a portion of the profits made in the business in which the deceased person was a partner, is not by reason only of such receipt a partner in the business or liable as such:

(*d*) The advance of money by way of loan to a person engaged or about to engage in any business on a contract with that person that the lender shall receive a rate of interest varying with the profits, or shall receive a share of the profits arising from carrying on the business, does not of itself make the lender a partner with the person or persons carrying on the business or liable as such. Provided that the contract is in writing, and signed by or on behalf of all the parties thereto:

(*e*) A person receiving by way of annuity or otherwise a portion of the profits of a business in consideration of the sale by him of the goodwill of the business is not by reason only of such receipt a partner in the business or liable as such.

3 Postponement of rights of person lending or selling in consideration of share of profits in case of insolvency

In the event of any person to whom money has been advanced by way of loan upon such a contract as is mentioned in the last foregoing section, or of any buyer of a goodwill in consideration of a share of the profits of the business, being adjudged a bankrupt, entering into an arrangement to pay his creditors less than twenty shillings in the pound, or dying in insolvent circumstances, the lender of the loan shall not be entitled to recover anything in respect of his loan, and the seller of the goodwill shall not be entitled to recover anything in respect of the share of profits contracted for, until the claims of the other creditors of the borrower or buyer for valuable consideration in money or money's worth have been satisfied.

4 Meaning of firm

(1) Persons who have entered into partnership with one another are for the purposes of this Act called collectively a firm, and the name under which their business is carried on is called the firm-name.

(2) In Scotland a firm is a legal person distinct from the partners of whom it is composed, but an individual partner may be charged on a

decree or diligence directed against the firm, and on payment of the debts is entitled to relief *pro ratâ* from the firm and its other members.

Relations of Partners to persons dealing with them

5 Power of partner to bind the firm

Every partner is an agent of the firm and his other partners for the purpose of the business of the partnership; and the acts of every partner who does any act for carrying on in the usual way business of the kind carried on by the firm of which he is a member bind the firm and his partners, unless the partner so acting has in fact no authority to act for the firm in the particular matter, and the person with whom he is dealing either knows that he has no authority, or does not know or believe him to be a partner.

6 Partners bound by acts on behalf of firm

An act or instrument relating to the business of the firm and done or executed in the firm-name, or in any other manner showing an intention to bind the firm, by any person thereto authorised, whether a partner or not, is binding on the firm and all the partners.

Provided that this section shall not affect any general rule of law relating to the execution of deeds or negotiable instruments.

7 Partner using credit of firm for private purposes

Where one partner pledges the credit of the firm for a purpose apparently not connected with the firm's ordinary course of business, the firm is not bound, unless he is in fact specially authorised by the other partners; but this section does not affect any personal liability incurred by an individual partner.

8 Effect of notice that firm will not be bound by acts of partner

If it has been agreed between the partners that any restriction shall be placed on the power of any one or more of them to bind the firm, no act done in contravention of the agreement is binding on the firm with respect to persons having notice of the agreement.

9 Liability of partners

Every partner in a firm is liable jointly with the other partners, and in Scotland severally also, for all debts and obligations of the firm incurred while he is a partner; and after his death his estate is also severally liable in a due course of administration for such debts and obligations, so far as they remain unsatisfied, but subject in England or Ireland to the prior payment of his separate debts.

10 Liability of the firm for wrongs

Where, by any wrongful act or omission of any partner acting in the ordinary course of the business of the firm, or with the authority of his co-partners, loss or injury is caused to any person not being a partner in the firm, or any penalty is incurred, the firm is liable therefor to the same extent as the partner so acting or omitting to act.

11 Misapplication of money or property received for or in custody of the firm

In the following cases; namely—

(*a*) Where one partner acting within the scope of his apparent authority receives the money or property of a third person and misapplies it; and

(*b*) Where a firm in the course of its business receives money or property of a third person, and the money or property so received is misapplied by one or more of the partners while it is in the custody of the firm;

the firm is liable to make good the loss.

12 Liability for wrongs joint and several

Every partner is liable jointly with his copartners and also severally for everything for which the firm while he is a partner therein becomes liable under either of the two last preceding sections.

13 Improper employment of trust-property for partnership purposes

If a partner, being a trustee, improperly employs trust-property in the business or on the account of the partnership, no other partner is liable for the trust-property to the persons beneficially interested therein.

Provided as follows:—

(1) This section shall not affect any liability incurred by any partner by reason of his having notice of a breach of trust; and

(2) Nothing in this section shall prevent trust money from being followed and recovered from the firm if still in its possession or under its control.

14 Persons liable by 'holding out'

(1) Every one who by words spoken or written or by conduct represents himself, or who knowingly suffers himself to be represented, as a partner in a particular firm, is liable as a partner to any one who has on the faith of any such representation given credit to the firm, whether the representation has or has not been made or communicated to the person so giving credit by or with the knowledge of the apparent partner making the representation or suffering it to be made.

(2) Provided that where after a partner's death the partnership business is continued in the old firm-name, the continued use of that name or of the deceased partner's name as part thereof shall not of itself make his

executors or administrators estate or effects liable for any partnership debts contracted after his death.

15 Admissions and representations of partners

An admission or representation made by any partner concerning the partnership affairs, and in the ordinary course of its business, is evidence against the firm.

16 Notice to acting partner to be notice to the firm

Notice to any partner who habitually acts in the partnership business of any matter relating to partnership affairs operates as notice to the firm, except in the case of a fraud on the firm committed by or with the consent of that partner.

17 Liabilities of incoming and outgoing partners

(1) A person who is admitted as a partner into an existing firm does not thereby become liable to the creditors of the firm for anything done before he became a partner.

(2) A partner who retires from a firm does not thereby cease to be liable for partnership debts or obligations incurred before his retirement.

(3) A retiring partner may be discharged from any existing liabilities, by an agreement to that effect between himself and the members of the firm as newly constituted and the creditors, and this agreement may be either express or inferred as a fact from the course of dealing between the creditors and the firm as newly constituted.

18 Revocation of continuing guaranty by change in firm

A continuing guaranty or cautionary obligation given either to a firm or to a third person in respect of the transactions of a firm is, in the absence of agreement to the contrary, revoked as to future transactions by any change in the constitution of the firm to which, or of the firm in respect of the transactions of which, the guaranty or obligation was given.

Relations of Partners to one another

19 Variation by consent of terms of partnership

The mutual rights and duties of partners, whether ascertained by agreement or defined by this Act, may be varied by the consent of all the partners, and such consent may be either express or inferred from a course of dealing.

20 Partnership property

(1) All property and rights and interests in property originally brought into the partnership stock or acquired, whether by purchase or otherwise, on account of the firm or for the purposes and in the course of the partnership business, are called in this Act partnership property, and must

be held and applied by the partners exclusively for the purposes of the partnership and in accordance with the partnership agreement.

(2) Provided that the legal estate or interest in any land, or in Scotland the title to and interest in any heritable estate, which belongs to the partnership shall devolve according to the nature and tenure thereof, and the general rules of law thereto applicable, but in trust, so far as necessary, for the persons beneficially interested in the land under this section.

(3) Where co-owners of an estate or interest in any land, or in Scotland of any heritable estate, not being itself partnership property, are partners as to profits made by the use of that land or estate, and purchase other land or estate out of the profits to be used in like manner, the land or estate so purchased belongs to them, in the absence of an agreement to the contrary, not as partners but as co-owners for the same respective estates and interests as are held by them in the land or estate first mentioned at the date of the purchase.

21 Property bought with partnership money

Unless the contrary intention appears, property bought with money belonging to the firm is deemed to have been bought on account of the firm.

22 Conversion into personal estate of land held as partnership property

Where land or any heritable interest therein has become partnership property, it shall, unless the contrary intention appears, be treated as between the partners (including the representatives of a deceased partner), and also as between the heirs of a deceased partner and his executors or administrators, as personal or moveable and not real or heritable estate.

23 Procedure against partnership property for a partner's separate judgment debt

(1) A writ of execution shall not issue against any partnership property except on a judgment against the firm.

(2) The High Court, or a judge thereof, or a county court, may, on the application by summons of any judgment creditor of a partner, make an order charging that partner's interest in the partnership property and profits with payment of the amount of the judgment debt and interest thereon, and may by the same or a subsequent order appoint a receiver of that partner's share of profits (whether already declared or accruing), and of any other money which may be coming to him in respect of the partnership, and direct all accounts and inquiries, and give all other orders and directions which might have been directed or given if the charge had been made in favour of the judgment creditor by the partner, or which the circumstances of the case may require.

(3) The other partner or partners shall be at liberty at any time to redeem the interest charged, or in case of a sale being directed, to purchase the same.

(4) This section shall apply in the case of a cost-book company as if the company were a partnership within the meaning of this Act.

(5) This section shall not apply to Scotland.

24 Rules as to interests and duties of partners subject to special agreement

The interests of partners in the partnership property and their rights and duties in relation to the partnership shall be determined, subject to any agreement express or implied between the partners, by the following rules:

(1) All the partners are entitled to share equally in the capital and profits of the business, and must contribute equally towards the losses whether of capital or otherwise sustained by the firm.

(2) The firm must indemnify every partner in respect of payments made and personal liabilities incurred by him—

(*a*) In the ordinary and proper conduct of the business of the firm; or,

(*b*) In or about anything necessarily done for the preservation of the business or property of the firm.

(3) A partner making, for the purpose of the partnership, any actual payment or advance beyond the amount of capital which he has agreed to subscribe, is entitled to interest at the rate of five per cent. per annum from the date of the payment or advance.

(4) A partner is not entitled, before the ascertainment of profits, to interest on the capital subscribed by him.

(5) Every partner may take part in the management of the partnership business.

(6) No partner shall be entitled to remuneration for acting in the partnership business.

(7) No person may be introduced as a partner without the consent of all existing partners.

(8) Any difference arising as to ordinary matters connected with the partnership business may be decided by a majority of the partners, but no change may be made in the nature of the partnership business without the consent of all existing partners.

(9) The partnership books are to be kept at the place of business of the partnership (or the principal place, if there is more than one), and every partner may, when he thinks fit, have access to and inspect and copy any of them.

25 Expulsion of partner

No majority of the partners can expel any partner unless a power to do so has been conferred by express agreement between the partners.

26 Retirement from partnership at will

(1) Where no fixed term has been agreed upon for the duration of the partnership, any partner may determine the partnership at any time on giving notice of his intention so to do to all the other partners.

(2) Where the partnership has originally been constituted by deed, a

notice in writing, signed by the partner giving it, shall be sufficient for this purpose.

27 Where partnership for term is continued over, continuance on old terms presumed

(1) Where a partnership entered into for a fixed term is continued after the term has expired, and without any express new agreement, the rights and duties of the partners remain the same as they were at the expiration of the term, so far as is consistent with the incidents of a partnership at will.

(2) A continuance of the business by the partners or such of them as habitually acted therein during the term, without any settlement or liquidation of the partnership affairs, is presumed to be a continuance of the partnership.

28 Duty of partners to render accounts, etc

Partners are bound to render true accounts and full information of all things affecting the partnership to any partner or his legal representatives.

29 Accountability of partners for private profits

(1) Every partner must account to the firm for any benefit derived by him without the consent of the other partners from any transaction concerning the partnership, or from any use by him of the partnership property name or business connexion.

(2) This section applies also to transactions undertaken after a partnership has been dissolved by the death of a partner, and before the affairs thereof have been completely wound up, either by any surviving partner or by the representatives of the deceased partner.

30 Duty of partner not to compete with firm

If a partner, without the consent of the other partners, carries on any business of the same nature as and competing with that of the firm, he must account for and pay over to the firm all profits made by him in that business.

31 Rights of assignee of share in partnership

(1) An assignment by any partner of his share in the partnership, either absolute or by way of mortgage or redeemable charge, does not, as against the other partners, entitle the assignee, during the continuance of the partnership, to interfere in the management or administration of the partnership business or affairs, or to require any accounts of the partnership transactions, or to inspect the partnership books, but entitles the assignee only to receive the share of profits to which the assigning partner would otherwise be entitled, and the assignee must accept the account of profits agreed to by the partners.

(2) In case of a dissolution of the partnership, whether as respects all the partners or as respects the assigning partner, the assignee is entitled to receive the share of the partnership assets to which the assigning partner is

entitled as between himself and the other partners, and, for the purpose of ascertaining that share, to an account as from the date of the dissolution.

Dissolution of Partnership, and its consequences

32 Dissolution by expiration or notice

Subject to any agreement between the partners a partnership is dissolved—

(*a*) If entered into for a fixed term, by the expiration of that term:

(*b*) If entered into for a single adventure or undertaking, by the termination of that adventure or undertaking:

(*c*) If entered into for an undefined time, by any partner giving notice to the other or others of his intention to dissolve the partnership.

In the last-mentioned case the partnership is dissolved as from the date mentioned in the notice as the date of dissolution, or, if no date is so mentioned, as from the date of the communication of the notice.

33 Dissolution by bankruptcy, death, or charge

(1) Subject to any agreement between the partners, every partnership is dissolved as regards all the partners by the death or bankruptcy of any partner.

(2) A partnership may, at the option of the other partners, be dissolved if any partner suffers his share of the partnership property to be charged under this Act for his separate debt.

34 Dissolution by illegality of partnership

A partnership is in every case dissolved by the happening of any event which makes it unlawful for the business of the firm to be carried on or for the members of the firm to carry it on in partnership.

35 Dissolution by the Court

On application by a partner the Court may decree a dissolution of the partnership in any of the following cases:

(*a*) [*Repealed.*]

(*b*) When a partner, other than the partner suing, becomes in any other way permanently incapable of performing his part of the partnership contract:

(*c*) When a partner, other than the partner suing, has been guilty of such conduct as, in the opinion of the Court, regard being had to the nature of the business, is calculated to prejudicially affect the carrying on of the business:

(*d*) When a partner, other than the partner suing, wilfully or persistently commits a breach of the partnership agreement, or otherwise so conducts himself in matters relating to the partnership business that it is not reasonably practicable for the other partner or partners to carry on the business in partnership with him:

(*e*) When the business of the partnership can only be carried on at a loss:

(*f*) Whenever in any case circumstances have arisen which, in the opinion of the Court, render it just and equitable that the partnership be dissolved.

36 Rights of persons dealing with firm against apparent members of firm

(1) Where a person deals with a firm after a change in its constitution he is entitled to treat all apparent members of the old firm as still being members of the firm until he has notice of the change.

(2) An advertisement in the London Gazette as to a firm whose principal place of business is in England or Wales, in the Edinburgh Gazette as to a firm whose principal place of business is in Scotland, and in the Dublin Gazette [*now the Belfast Gazette*] as to a firm whose principal place of business is in Ireland, shall be notice as to persons who had not dealings with the firm before the date of the dissolution or change so advertised.

(3) The estate of a partner who dies, or who becomes bankrupt, or of a partner who, not having been known to the person dealing with the firm to be a partner, retires from the firm, is not liable for partnership debts contracted after the date of the death, bankruptcy, or retirement respectively.

37 Right of partners to notify dissolution

On the dissolution of a partnership or retirement of a partner any partner may publicly notify the same, and may require the other partner or partners to concur for that purpose in all necessary or proper acts, if any, which cannot be done without his or their concurrence.

38 Continuing authority of partners for purposes of winding up

After the dissolution of a partnership the authority of each partner to bind the firm, and the other rights and obligations of the partners, continue notwithstanding the dissolution so far as may be necessary to wind up the affairs of the partnership, and to complete transactions begun but unfinished at the time of the dissolution, but not otherwise.

Provided that the firm is in no case bound by the acts of a partner who has become bankrupt; but this proviso does not affect the liability of any person who has after the bankruptcy represented himself or knowingly suffered himself to be represented as a partner of the bankrupt.

39 Rights of partners as to application of partnership property

On the dissolution of a partnership every partner is entitled, as against the other partners in the firm, and all persons claiming through them in respect of their interests as partners, to have the property of the partnership applied in payment of the debts and liabilities of the firm, and to have the surplus assets after such payment applied in payment of what may be due to the partners respectively after deducting what may be due from them as partners to the firm; and for that purpose any partner or his representatives may on the termination of the partnership apply to the Court to wind up the business and affairs of the firm.

40 Apportionment of premium where partnership prematurely dissolved

Where one partner has paid a premium to another on entering into a partnership for a fixed term, and the partnership is dissolved before the expiration of that term otherwise than by the death of a partner, the Court may order the repayment of the premium, or of such part thereof as it thinks just, having regard to the terms of the partnership contract and to the length of time during which the partnership has continued; unless

(*a*) the dissolution is, in the judgment of the Court, wholly or chiefly due to the misconduct of the partner who paid the premium, or

(*b*) the partnership has been dissolved by an agreement containing no provision for a return of any part of the premium.

41 Rights where partnership dissolved for fraud or misrepresentation

Where a partnership contract is rescinded on the ground of the fraud or misrepresentation of one of the parties thereto, the party entitled to rescind is, without prejudice to any other right, entitled—

(*a*) to a lien on, or right of retention of, the surplus of the partnership assets, after satisfying the partnership liabilities, for any sum of money paid by him for the purchase of a share in the partnership and for any capital contributed by him, and is

(*b*) to stand in the place of the creditors of the firm for any payments made by him in respect of the partnership liabilities, and

(*c*) to be indemnified by the person guilty of the fraud or making the representation against all the debts and liabilities of the firm.

42 Right of outgoing partner in certain cases to share profits made after dissolution

(1) Where any member of a firm has died or otherwise ceased to be a partner, and the surviving or continuing partners carry on the business of the firm with its capital or assets without any final settlement of accounts as between the firm and the outgoing partner or his estate, then, in the absence of any agreement to the contrary, the outgoing partner or his estate is entitled at the option of himself or his representatives to such share of the profits made since the dissolution as the Court may find to be attributable to the use of his share of the partnership assets, or to interest at the rate of five per cent. per annum on the amount of his share of the partnership assets.

(2) Provided that where by the partnership contract an option is given to surviving or continuing partners to purchase the interest of a deceased or outgoing partner, and that option is duly exercised, the estate of the deceased partner, or the outgoing partner or his estate, as the case may be, is not entitled to any further or other share of profits; but if any partner assuming to act in exercise of the option does not in all material respects

comply with the terms thereof, he is liable to account under the foregoing provisions of this section.

43 Retiring or deceased partner's share to be a debt

Subject to any agreement between the partners, the amount due from surviving or continuing partners to an outgoing partner or the representatives of a deceased partner in respect of the outgoing or deceased partner's share is a debt accruing at the date of the dissolution or death.

44 Rule for distribution of assets on final settlement of accounts

In settling accounts between the partners after a dissolution of partnership, the following rules shall, subject to any agreement, be observed:

(*a*) Losses, including losses and deficiencies of capital, shall be paid first out of profits, next out of capital, and lastly, if necessary, by the partners individually in the proportion in which they were entitled to share profits:

(*b*) The assets of the firm including the sums, if any, contributed by the partners to make up losses or deficiencies of capital, shall be applied in the following manner and order:

1. In paying the debts and liabilities of the firm to persons who are not partners therein:
2. In paying to each partner rateably what is due from the firm to him for advances as distinguished from capital:
3. In paying to each partner rateably what is due from the firm to him in respect of capital:
4. The ultimate residue, if any, shall be divided among the partners in the proportion in which the profits are divisible.

Supplemental

45 Definitions of 'court' and 'business'

In this Act, unless the contrary intention appears—

The expression 'court' includes every court and judge having jurisdiction in the case;

The expression 'business' includes every trade, occupation, or profession.

46 Saving for rules of equity and common law

The rules of equity and of common law applicable to partnership shall continue in force except so far as they are inconsistent with the express provisions of this Act.

47 Provision as to bankruptcy in Scotland

(1) In the application of this Act to Scotland the bankruptcy of a firm

or of an individual shall mean sequestration under the Bankruptcy (Scotland) Acts, and also in the case of an individual the issue against him of a decree of cessio bonorum.

(2) Nothing in this Act shall alter the rules of the law of Scotland relating to the bankruptcy of a firm or of the individual partners thereof.

48, 49 [*Repealed.*]

50 Short title

This Act may be cited as the Partnership Act, 1890.

SCHEDULE—[*Repealed.*]

Appendix 2

Inland Revenue Statement of Practice Capital Gains Tax: Partnerships (17 January 1975)

The Board of Inland Revenue have had discussions with the Law Society and the Allied Accountancy Bodies on the capital gains tax treatment of partnerships. This statement sets out a number of points of general practice which have been agreed.

1 Nature of the asset liable to tax

Section 45(7), Finance Act 1965 [*now section 60 of the Capital Gains Tax Act 1979*], treats any partnership dealings in chargeable assets for capital gains tax purposes as dealings by the individual partners rather than by the firm as such. Each partner has therefore to be regarded as owning a fractional share of each of the partnership assets and not for this purpose an interest in the partnership.

Where it is necessary to ascertain the market value of a partner's share in a partnership asset for capital gains tax purposes, it will be taken as a fraction of the value of the total partnership interest in the asset without any discount for the size of his share. If, for example, a partnership owned all the issued shares in a company, the value of the interest in that holding of a partner with a one-tenth share would be one-tenth of the value of the partnership's 100 per cent holding.

2 Disposals of assets by a partnership

Where an asset is disposed of by a partnership to an outside party each of the partners will be treated as disposing of his fractional share of the asset. Similarly if a partnership makes a part disposal of an asset each partner will be treated as making a part disposal of his fractional share. In computing gains or losses the proceeds of disposal will be allocated between the partners in the ratio of their shares in asset surpluses at the time of the disposal. Where this is not specifically laid down the allocation will follow the actual destination of the surplus as shown in the partnership accounts; regard will of course have to be paid to any agreement outside the accounts. If the surplus is not allocated among the partners but, for example, put to a common reserve, regard will be had to the ordinary profit-sharing ratio in the absence of a specified asset-surplus-sharing ratio. Expenditure on the acquisition of assets by a partnership will be allocated between the partners in the same way at the time of the acquisition. This allocation may require adjustment, however, if there is a subsequent change in the partnership sharing ratios (see paragraph 4).

3 Partnership assets divided in kind among the partners

Where a partnership distributes an asset in kind to one or more of the partners, for example on dissolution, a partner who receives the asset will not be regarded as disposing of his fractional share in it. A computation will first be necessary of the gains which would be chargeable on the individual partners if the asset had been disposed of at its current market value. Where this results in a gain being attributed to a partner not receiving the asset the gain will be charged at the time of the distribution of the asset. Where, however, the gain is allocated to a partner receiving the asset concerned there will be no charge on distribution. Instead, his capital gains tax cost to be carried forward will be the market value of the asset at the date of distribution as reduced by the amount of his gain. The same principles will be applied where the computation results in a loss.

4 Changes in partnership sharing ratios

An occasion of charge also arises when there is a change in partnership sharing ratios including changes arising from a partner joining or leaving the partnership. In these circumstances a partner who reduces or gives up his share in asset surpluses will be treated as disposing of part or the whole of his share in each of the partnership assets and a partner who increases his share will be treated as making a similar acquisition. Subject to the qualifications mentioned at 6 and 7 below the disposal consideration will be a fraction (equal to the fractional share changing hands) of the current balance sheet value of each chargeable asset provided that there is no direct payment of consideration outside the partnership. Where no adjustment is made through the partnership accounts (for example, by revaluation of the assets coupled with a corresponding increase or decrease in the partner's current or capital account at some date between the partner's acquisition and the reduction in his share) the disposal is treated as made for a consideration equal to his capital gains tax cost and thus there will be neither a chargeable gain nor an allowable loss at that point. A partner whose share reduces will carry forward a smaller proportion of cost to set against a subsequent disposal of the asset and a partner whose share increases will carry forward a larger proportion of cost.

The general rules in paragraph 7 of Schedule 6, Finance Act 1965 [*now section 35 of the Capital Gains Tax Act 1979*], for apportioning the total acquisition cost on a part disposal of an asset will not be applied in the case of a partner reducing his asset-surplus share. Instead, the cost of the part disposed of will be calculated on a fractional basis.

5 Adjustments through the accounts

Where a partnership asset is revalued a partner will be credited in his current or capital account with a sum equal to his fractional share of the increase in value. An upward revaluation of chargeable assets is not itself an occasion of charge. If, however, there were to be a subsequent reduction in the partner's asset-surplus share, the effect would be to reduce his potential liability to capital gains tax on the eventual disposal of the assets without an equivalent reduction of the credit he has received in the accounts. Consequently at the time of the reduction in sharing ratio he will be regarded as disposing of the fractional share of the partnership asset represented by the difference between his old and his new share for a consideration equal to that fraction of the increased value at the revaluation. The partner whose share correspondingly increases will have his acquisition cost to be carried forward for the asset increased by the same amount. The same principles will be applied in the case of a downward revaluation.

6 Payments outside the accounts

Where on a change of partnership sharing ratios payments are made directly between two or more partners outside the framework of the partnership accounts, the payments represent consideration for the disposal of the whole or part of a partner's share in partnership assets in addition to any consideration calculated on the bases described in 4 and 5 above. Often such payments will be for goodwill not included in the balance sheet. In such cases the partner receiving the payment will have no capital gains tax cost to set against it unless he made a similar payment for his share in the asset (for example, on entering the partnership) or elects to have the market value at 6th April 1965 treated as his acquisition cost. The partner making the payment will only be allowed to deduct the amount in computing gains or losses on a subsequent disposal of his share in the asset. He will be able to claim a loss when he finally leaves the partnership or when his share is reduced provided that he then receives either no consideration or a lesser consideration for his share of the asset. Where the payment clearly constitutes payment for a share in assets included in the partnership accounts, the partner receiving it will be able to deduct the amount of the partnership acquisition cost represented by the fraction he is disposing of. Special treatment, as outlined in 7 below, may be necessary for transfers between persons not at arm's-length.

7 Transfers between persons not at arm's-length

Where no payment is made either through or outside the accounts in connection with a change in partnership sharing ratio, a capital gains tax charge will only arise if the transaction is otherwise than by way of a bargain made at arm's-length and falls therefore within Section 22(4) (a), Finance Act 1965 [*now section 19(3)(a) of the Capital Gains Tax Act 1979*], as extended by paragraph 17(2) of Schedule 7, Finance Act 1965 [*now section 62(2) of the Capital Gains Tax Act 1979*], for transactions between connected persons. Under paragraph 21(4) of that Schedule [*now section 63(4) of the Capital Gains Tax Act 1979*] transfers of partnership assets between partners are not regarded as transactions between connected persons if they are pursuant to bona fide commercial arrangements. This treatment will also be given to transactions between an incoming partner and the existing partners.

Where the partners (including incoming partners) are connected other than by partnership (for example, father and son) or are otherwise not at arm's-length (for example, uncle and nephew) the transfer of a share in the partnership assets may fall to be treated as having been made at market value. Market value will not be substituted, however, if nothing would have been paid had the parties been at arm's-length. Similarly if consideration of less than market value passes between partners connected other than by partnership or otherwise not at arm's-length, the transfer will only be regarded as having been made for full market value if the consideration actually paid was less than that which would have been paid by parties at arm's-length. Where a transfer has to be treated as if it had taken place for market value, the deemed disposal proceeds will fall to be treated in the same way as payments outside the accounts.

8 Annuities provided by partnerships

A lump sum which is paid to a partner on leaving the partnership or on a reduction of his share in the partnership represents consideration for the disposal by the partner concerned of the whole or part of his share in the partnership assets and will be subject to the rules in 6 above. The same treatment will apply when a partnership buys a purchased life annuity for a partner, the measure of the consideration being the actual cost of the annuity.

Where a partnership makes annual payments to a retired partner (whether under covenant or not) the capitalised value of the annuity will only be treated as consideration for the disposal of his share in the partnership assets under paragraph 2(3) of Schedule 6, Finance Act 1965 [*now section 31(3) of the Capital Gains Tax Act 1979*], if it is more than can be regarded as a reasonable recognition of the past contribution of work and effort by the partner to the partnership. Provided that the former partner had been in the partnership for at least 10 years an annuity will be regarded as reasonable for this purpose if it is no more than two-thirds of his average share of the profits in the best 3 of the last 7 years in which he was required to devote substantially the whole of his time to acting as a partner. In arriving at a partner's share of the profits regard will be had to the partnership profits assessed before deduction of any capital allowances or charges. The 10 year period will include any period during which the partner was a member of another firm whose business has been merged with that of the present firm. For lesser periods the following fractions will be used instead of the two-thirds:

Complete years in partnership	*Fraction*
1–5	1/60 for each year
6	8/60
7	16/60
8	24/60
9	32/60

Where the capitalised value of an annuity is treated as consideration received by the retired partner, it will also be regarded as allowable expenditure by the remaining partners on the acquisition of their fractional shares in partnership assets from him.

[The Board have now agreed that this practice will be extended to certain cases in which a lump sum is paid in addition to an annuity. Where the aggregate of the annuity and one-ninth of the lump sum does not exceed the appropriate fraction (as indicated in the Statement) of the retired partner's average share of the profits, the capitalised value of the annuity will not be treated as consideration in the hands of the retired partner. The lump sum, however, will continue to be so treated.

This extension of the practice will be applied to all cases in which the liability has not been finally determined at the date of this Notice [*12 January 1979*].]

9 Mergers

When the members of two or more existing partnerships come together to form a new one, the capital gains tax treatment will follow the same lines as that for changes in partnership sharing ratios. If gains arise for reasons similar to those covered in 5 and 6 above, it may be possible for roll-over relief under Section 33, Finance Act 1965 [*now sections 115–121 of the Capital Gains Tax Act 1979*], to be claimed by any partner continuing in the partnership insofar as he disposes of part of his share in the assets of the old firm and acquires a share in other assets put into the 'merged' firm. Where, however, in such cases the consideration given for the shares in chargeable assets acquired is less than the consideration for those disposed of, relief will be restricted under Section 33(2) [*now section 116(1) of the Capital Gains Tax Act 1979*].

10 Shares acquired in stages

Where a share in a partnership is acquired in stages wholly after 5th April 1965, the acquisition costs of the various chargeable assets will be calculated by pooling the expenditure relating to each asset. Where a share built up in stages was acquired wholly or partly before 6th April 1965 the rules in paragraph 26 of Schedule 6, Finance Act 1965 [*now paragraph 13 of Schedule 5 to the Capital Gains Tax Act 1979*], will normally be followed to identify the acquisition cost of the share in each asset which is disposed of on the occasion of a reduction in the partnership's share; i.e., the disposal will normally be identified with shares acquired on a 'first in, first out' basis. Special consideration will be given, however, to any case in which this rule appears to produce an unreasonable result when applied to temporary changes in the shares in a partnership, for example those occurring when a partner's departure and a new partner's arrival are out of step by a few months.

11 Elections under Schedule 11, Finance Act 1968

Where the assets disposed of are quoted securities eligible for a pooling election under Schedule 11, Finance Act 1968, [*now paragraphs 4–7 of Schedule 5 to the Capital Gains Tax Act 1979*], partners will be allowed to make separate elections in respect of shares or fixed interest securities held by the partnership as distinct from shares or securities which they hold on a personal basis. Each partner will have a separate right of election for his proportion of the partnership securities and the time limit for the purposes of Schedule 11 will run from the earlier of—

(*a*) the first relevant disposal of shares or securities by the partnership, and

(*b*) the first reduction of the particular partner's share in the partnership assets after 19th March 1968.

Where this time limit expired before today, the Board will consider sympathetically a request for extension within the next 2 years if the liability has not been finally determined and the tax paid.

12 Transitional arrangements

The practices set out in this statement will be applied to all capital gains tax assessments after today. Where tax liabilities have already been settled on other reasonable bases the assessments will not be upset. Often gains and losses on previous disposals will have been computed on a different basis and the acquisition costs allocated as a result to partners to set against future disposals will be different from those which would have arisen had the new practices been followed. Such costs will only be recalculated in exceptional circumstances.

Appendix 3

Partnership Deed

The following partnership deed is an abridged version of that appearing in Appendix A to *Organisation and Management of a Solicitor's Practice*, edited by P Purton and D Andrews and published by Oyez Longman (looseleaf).

THIS PARTNERSHIP DEED is dated
and is made between:
(1) to ( ) the persons whose names are stated in column (1) of Schedule 1 ('the [Existing] Partners') all being Solicitors of
and
[(2) to ( ) the persons whose names are stated in column (1) of Schedule 2 ('the New Partners') all being Solicitors of]

WHEREAS it is the intention of the Partners to practise in partnership together on the following terms:
OR [(A) The Existing Partners have as profit-sharing partners (together with the New Partners and others as salaried partners) carried on business as Solicitors at

under the firm name of]

[(B)] The New Partners became profit-sharing partners on 19]

[(C)] Although the partnership constituted by this Deed is for a period of [ ] years nevertheless it is the intention of the parties hereto to continue in partnership from [ ] year period to [ ] year period subject only to the incidence of death or retirement.]

NOW THIS DEED WITNESSETH as follows:

1 Interpretation

(A) In this Deed the following expressions have the following meanings:

'the Partnership'	the partnership constituted by this Deed
'the Partnership Business'	the business and profession of Solicitors carried on hereunder

['the Old Partnership'	the partnership referred to in Recital (A) hereto as carried on until 19]
['the Partners'	the Existing Partners and the New Partners and such other persons as may become profit-sharing partners with them during the period of the Partnership for so long in each case as they remain profit-sharing partners in the Partnership]
'Profit-Sharing Group'	a group of the Partners having a like share in the profits of the Partnership
'the Salaried Partners'	the persons whose names are stated in Schedule 3 and any other persons for the time being admitted into and continuing in partnership with the Partners as salaried partners
'the Consultants'	the persons whose names are stated in Schedule 4
'Year of the Partnership'	the period commencing on 19 and ending on 19 and each successive period of 12 months thereafter commencing on [ ] and ending on [ ] during the continuance of the Partnership
'the Taxes Act'	the Income and Corporation Taxes Act 1970

(B) For all purposes of this Deed seniority of the Partners shall be determined according to the order in which their respective names appear in Schedules 1 and 2.

(C) References in this Deed to Clauses, sub-clauses and Schedules are to Clauses and sub-clauses of and Schedules to this Deed.

(D) The headings to Clauses and Schedules are for ease of reference only and shall not affect the interpretation thereof.

(E) References in this Deed to statutory provisions shall be construed as references to those provisions as respectively amended or re-enacted (whether before or after the date hereof) from time to time and shall include any provisions of which they are re-enactments (whether with or without modification)

2 Effective date

The provisions of this Deed shall be deemed to have taken effect as on and from [19] in substitution for and to the exclusion of all previous deeds and agreements between any of the Partners (save as otherwise expressly provided in this Deed) [and save that such former deeds and agreements shall continue to regulate the entitlement of the Existing Partners to any undistributed profits of any previous Partnership).]

3 Firm name and location of practice

The Partners shall practise in partnership as Solicitors under the firm name of
[ ]
(or such other name as the Partners may hereafter agree) at [
]
aforesaid and/or at such other place or places as the Partners may from time to time decide.

4 The salaried partners

The Partners shall be deemed to have admitted into partnership with them on and from [19] the Salaried Partners and none of the Salaried Partners shall be required to contribute any capital to the Partnership or be required to bear any part of the losses (if any).

5 Period of the partnership

(A) The period of the Partnership shall be [ ] years from [19] to [19].

(B) The death, retirement, expulsion or bankruptcy of a Partner shall not determine the Partnership between the other Partners but without prejudice to the generality of this Clause the parties hereto shall review the provisions of this Deed whenever the admission of a new profit-sharing partner into the Partnership is being contemplated.

6 Partnership capital

(A) The initial capital of the Partnership shall consist of the sum of [£] which has been contributed by the Partners in cash or otherwise as the Partners may have agreed in the proportions specified in column (2) of Schedule[s] 1 [and 2] together with such further cash capital (if any) as the Partners may from time to time agree to be required (in addition to any loan capital) for the purposes of the Partnership and which shall be provided (except as may from time to time be otherwise agreed by the Partners) in the proportions in which the Partners are for the time being entitled to share in the profits of the Partnership.

[(B) The said sum of [£] and any further capital provided by the Partners shall carry interest at the rate of [ ] per cent per annum to be payable [half-yearly] in arrears on [ ] at [ ] or at such other rate and payable at such other times as the Partners shall from time to time decide.

7 Shares in profits and losses

The shares of the Partners in the profits and losses (if any) of the Partnership shall be as specified in column (3) of Schedule[s] 1 [and 2] or such other shares as may from time to time be agreed by the Partners.

8 Consultancy agreements

The Partners shall continue the existing Consultancy Agreements (as already amended in respect of the consultancy fees payable thereunder) with the Consultants. The amounts of the consultancy fees payable under all of such Consultancy Agreements shall be reviewed [annually] in respect of each Year of the Partnership.

9 Control and management of the partnership

The control and management of the Partnership shall remain in the hands of the Partners and save as hereinafter provided the Salaried Partners shall not be entitled to take part therein.

10 Circulation of agendas and other information

All Agendas and Minutes of Partners' Meetings and balance sheets and profit and loss accounts shall be circulated to all Partners.

11 Partnership accounts and partners' drawings

The Accounts of the Partnership in respect of each Year of the Partnership shall be made up yearly as at the close of business on the last day of such year. Each Partner may draw on account of his share of profits to such extent as may be decided by the Partners from time to time.

12 Bank accounts and application of partnership moneys

(A) The Bankers of the Partnership shall be [ ] Bank Limited or such other bankers as the Partners shall agree upon both for the moneys of clients for the time being in the keeping of the Partnership and for the moneys of the Partnership.

(B) All moneys of the Partnership shall be paid to the Bankers of the Partnership to the credit of the Partnership and the Partners shall make such regulations as they from time to time see fit for opening, operating or closing the bank accounts of the Partnership and for providing the moneys required for current expenses.

(C) All outgoings incurred for or in carrying on the Partnership Business and all losses and damages which shall happen or be incurred in relation to the business shall be paid out of the moneys and profits of the Partnership and in case of deficiency shall be contributed by the Partners in the shares in which they shall for the time being be respectively entitled to the profits of the Partnership.

13 Conduct of the partnership business

Each Partner shall diligently employ himself in the Partnership Business and carry on and conduct the same for the greatest advantage of the Partnership.

14 Holidays

Each Partner shall be entitled to [ ] weeks' holiday in aggregate in each Year of the Partnership and shall be obliged to take a minimum of [ ] weeks' holiday in aggregate in each Year of the Partnership.

15 Restrictions on engagement of partners in other businesses

(A) Each Partner may retain and appropriate to his own use the benefit of any directorship or other office of profit which he may hold at the commencement of the Partnership and which he is then appropriating to his own use but save as aforesaid no Partner shall accept or hold any directorship or other office of profit or either alone or in conjunction with any other person either directly or indirectly engage in any profession or trade or business (otherwise than as a shareholder) without the consent of the other Partners.

(B) Except with the consent of the other Partners no Partner shall during the Partnership act as Solicitor for or on behalf of any person or undertake any professional business or (except pursuant to sub-clause (A) of this Clause) hold or accept any office usually held by Solicitors otherwise than for the benefit of the Partnership.

(C) Every Partner shall account to the Partnership for any fees, remuneration or profits obtained by him from any directorship, office, engagement or business which is held or undertaken by him in breach of the provisions of this Clause or (unless the other Partners otherwise decide) which is held or undertaken by him with the consent of the other Partners under this Clause.

16 Other restrictions on partners

No Partner shall:

(A) undertake the prosecution or defence of any action or suit or transact any professional business after being required not to do so by a decision of the Partners, or

(B) without the previous consent of the Partners hire or dismiss any employee or take any articled clerk, or

(C) without the previous consent of the Partners assign his share or interest in the Partnership or any part thereof or give to any person an interest therein or employ any of the moneys goods or effects of the Partnership or engage the credit of the Partnership except upon the account or for the use of the Partnership, or

(D) without the previous consent of the Partners release any debt or liability to the Partnership (other than a debt or liability not exceeding in any one case the aggregate of £[ ] and any Value Added Tax chargeable thereon) or enter into any bond or became bail surety or security with or for any person (other than a Partner) or do or knowingly suffer anything whereby or by reason whereof the capital or effects of the Partnership may be seized attached or taken in execution.

17 Partners' debts and engagements

Every Partner shall during the Partnership pay his present and future separate debts and at all times indemnify the other Partners and each of them and the capital and effects of the Partnership against his said debts and engagements and against all actions suits claims and demands on account thereof.

18 [Compulsory] provision for retirement and life assurance

(A) Subject to the provisions of sub-clauses (C) and (E) of this Clause each of the Partners [shall be obliged] [is encouraged] to enter into and maintain a retirement annuity contract within Section 226 of the Taxes Act and to pay thereunder in each Year of the Partnership a premium of not less than the maximum amount in respect of which relief may for the time being be claimed by such Partner under Section 227 of the Taxes Act. Provided that if the Partners so decide the said Section 227 shall be read and construed for the purpose of applying this sub-clause as if there were substituted for the sum and/or the percentage specified in paragraphs (a) and (b) respectively of sub-section (1A) of such section such lesser sum (not being less than [£] and/or such lesser percentage (not being less than 17½%) as the Partners shall from time to time stipulate

[(B) Each of the Partners who was born on or after [ ] shall be obliged to enter into and maintain a contract of term life assurance on his own life to the age of sixty-five]

[(C) In the case of any Partner maintaining such a contract of term life assurance as is mentioned under sub-clause (B) of this Clause the minimum premium required to be paid by him in each Year of the Partnership pursuant to sub-clause (A) of this Clause shall (notwithstanding the provisions of that sub-clause) be reduced by the amount of his term life assurance premium]

(D) The aggregate of the minimum premium required to be paid by any Partner in each Year of the Partnership pursuant to sub-clause (A) of this Clause (as reduced under sub-clause (C) but ignoring any variation under sub-clause (E)) and the amount (if any) of the premium required to be paid by him in that year to sub-clause (B) of this Clause is hereafter referred to as such Partner's 'total standard premium'

(E) The obligations under sub-clauses (A) (B) and (C) of this Clause shall be varied as follows in respect of any of the Partners as regards any Year of the Partnership which falls within the period of [ ] years commencing with the date on which he shall have first become a profit-sharing partner in the Partnership or (where he was a profit-sharing partner in the Old Partnership) in the Old Partnership:

(i) in any Year of the Partnership coinciding with the first of such [ ] years he shall have no obligation under sub-clause (A) of this Clause

(ii) in any Year of the Partnership coinciding with the second or third of such [ ] years the obligations under sub-clauses (A) and (B) of this Clause shall apply to him subject to the variation that the minimum premium which he is obliged to pay in that year pursuant to sub-clause (A) of this Clause (before taking account of any reduction under sub-clause (C)) shall be not less than whichever is the greater of:

(*a*) [ ] of his gross income from the Partnership in the preceding year and

(*b*) one-half of the amount of his total standard premium.

(F) To the extent that the profits of the Partnership in each Year of the Partnership are sufficient for the purpose there shall be set aside out of such profits a sum equal to the aggregate of the respective amounts payable in that year by all of the Partners by way of premiums under the retirement annuity contracts and contracts of term life assurance maintained by them as aforesaid (but not exceeding in the case of any of the Partners the amount of his total standard premium) and each of the Partners shall be entitled to draw from such sum on account of his share of profits by such instalments on such dates in that year as the Partners shall specify and to apply in or towards payment of, or reimbursement of the amount of, the premiums payable by him in that year under the retirement annuity contract and contract of term life assurance entered into by him as aforesaid an amount equal to the total of such premiums or the amount of his total standard premium (whichever shall be the less)

(G) In any event that the profits of the Partnership in any Year of the Partnership shall be insufficient to set aside the sum referred to in sub-clause (F) of this Clause or in the event that any material change shall be made by law in the treatment afforded for tax purposes to retirement annuities and term life assurance and the premiums payable in respect of contracts for the same the Partners shall have power to make such changes to the provisions of this Clause as may in their opinion be desirable in the interests of the Partners

(H) Whilst it is at the discretion of each Partner as to the exercise in relation to any retirement annuity contract entered into by him as aforesaid of any right or option for the payment of any annuity to his widow or for the payment of a lump sum in commutation of any part of the annuity payable to him each Partner shall assume that (save as specified in Clauses 19 to 24) all obligations to him on the part of the other Partners shall cease on his retirement and shall recognise that it is his own responsibility to ensure that due provision is made for his widow and other dependants.

19 Annuities to partners' dependants in the event of death

(A) If any Partner dies during the continuance of the Partnership leaving a dependant or dependants surviving him the continuing Partners shall pay to such dependant or (if more than one) to such dependants in such proportions as the continuing Partners in their absolute discretion decide (with power to vary such proportions at any time and from time to time) an annuity of or amounting in the aggregate to £[ ] (subject to increase as hereinafter provided) during the period from the date of the deceased Partner's death to:

(i) the date when the deceased Partner would have attained the age of sixty-five years or

(ii) the expiry of ten years from the date of the deceased Partner's death or

(iii) the date when there shall remain no dependant of the deceased partner whichever first occurs

(B) The amount of any annuity payable in pursuance of this Clause shall be reviewed as at the date of the deceased Partner's death and each anniversary thereof within the period during which such annuity is payable and the figure of £[ ] specified in sub-clause (A) of this Clause shall be increased with effect from that date in proportion to one half of any increase in the cost of living since [19] such increase in the cost of living being established by reference to the All Items Cost of Living Index of Retail Prices prepared by the Department of Employment (or other official cost of living index published in place thereof) as most recently published before [19] and as most recently published before the date of the said review.

20 Annuities to partners in the event of permanent incapacity

(A) If any Partner ceases to be a Partner by reason of his becoming permanently incapacitated by ill-health (including mental disorder and injury) from attending to the Partnership Business the continuing Partners shall pay to him an annuity equal to the amount specified in sub-clause (C) of this Clause during the period from the date when he ceases to be a Partner to the date of his death or the date when he attains the age of sixty-five years whichever first occurs.

(B) If the outgoing Partner shall die while any annuity is payable to him pursuant to sub-clause (A) of this Clause and if he shall leave a dependant or dependants surviving him the continuing Partners shall pay to such dependant or (if more than one) to such dependants in such proportions as the continuing Partners in their absolute discretion decide (with power to vary such proportions at any time and from time to time) the amount specified in sub-clause (C) of this Clause during the period from the date of the outgoing Partner's death to

(i) the date when the outgoing Partner would have attained the age of sixty-five years or

(ii) the date when there shall remain no dependant of the outgoing Partner whichever first occurs.

(C) The amount referred to in sub-clauses (A) and (B) of this Clause by reference to which any annuity payable thereunder is to be computed shall be whichever is the smallest of the following:

(i) the limit specified in Section 16(2) of the Finance Act 1974 as applied to the outgoing Partner; and

(ii) [ ] per cent of the net profits of the Partnership for the completed Year of the Partnership next preceding the year in which the annuity is payable (years being computed for this purpose from the commencement of the period during which the annuity is payable); and

(iii) [ ]

(D) In this Clause the expression 'net profits of the Partnership' means the net revenue profits of the Partnership as shown in its profit and loss account computed after taking into account all charges provisions and credits inclusive of those made for interest on capital and depreciation of assets but exclusive of any deduction or provision for taxation.

[21 Payment and commutation of annuities

(A) Every annuity payable pursuant to Clause 19 or Clause 20

(i) shall accrue on a day to day basis;

(ii) shall be payable without any deduction except for income tax; and

(iii) shall be paid by equal quarterly instalments the first such instalment to be paid at the end of the first three months of the period during which the annuity is payable.

(B) If the Partnership business is dissolved or discontinued (other than for tax purposes or for purposes of amalgamation or reconstruction) at a time when any annuity is payable or contingently payable pursuant to Clause 19 or Clause 20 the continuing Partners shall pay in lieu thereof a lump sum equal to the capital value thereof as found by actuarial valuation which sum (where the annuity was payable or contingently payable to the dependants for the time being in existence of a deceased or outgoing Partner) to be divided between such dependants in such proportions as the continuing Partners in their absolute discretion decide.]

[22 Liability in respect of annuities

The continuing Partners from time to time and for the time being shall be jointly and severally liable to pay any annuity or lump sum which is payable pursuant to Clause 19, Clause 20 or Clause 21 but as between themselves they shall bear the amount of every such payment in the proportion in which they are entitled for the time being to share inter se in the profits of the Partnership.]

[23 Meaning of 'dependant'

In Clauses 19, 20 and 21 hereof expression 'dependant' in relation to any deceased or outgoing Partner shall mean any individual (including the spouse and any child of such Partner) who in the opinion of the continuing Partners is financially dependent on such Partner at the date of his death for the ordinary necessities of life provided that any such individual shall be deemed to continue to be a dependant only for as long as in the opinion of the continuing Partners he or she shall be in need of financial assistance.]

24 Payments to outgoing partners

(A) Upon any Partner dying or in accordance with a decision of the

Partners retiring or otherwise ceasing to be a Partner ('outgoing partner') during the continuation of the Partnership or at the termination thereof in circumstances where a majority in number of the Partners continue in partnership thereafter there shall be paid to the outgoing partner or his personal representatives:

(i) the amount of his capital at the date of his ceasing to be a Partner ('the relevant date') with interest on capital both accrued due to the relevant date and from the relevant date up to the date of payment, such date of payment to be as soon as practicable after the relevant date;*

(ii) his share of undrawn profits up to the relevant date which in respect of the Year of the Partnership in which he ceases to be a Partner shall be calculated in accordance with the formula:

$$\frac{A}{100} \times \frac{B}{C} \times D$$

where:

A equals the percentage of profits to which he was entitled at the relevant date;

B equals the number of days from the start of the Year of the Partnership in question to the relevant date;

C equals the number of days in the Year of the Partnership in question; and

D equals the profits of the Partnership for the Year of the Partnership in question; and

(iii) the amount standing to the credit of his current account with the Partnership in respect of any Year of the Partnership ended prior to the start of the Year of the Partnership in which he ceases to be a Partner.

(B) The continuing Partners shall be entitled to retain out of any amounts payable under paragraphs (ii) and (iii) of sub-clause (A) of this Clause a sum sufficient to discharge any tax for which the Partnership may be liable in respect of the same or in respect of any period prior to the relevant date.

(C) Subject as provided in sub-clause (B) of this Clause, the amount payable under paragraph (iii) of sub-clause (A) of this Clause shall be paid as soon as practicable after the relevant date and the amount payable under paragraph (ii) of sub-clause (A) of this Clause shall be paid as soon as practicable after completion of the audited accounts of the Partnership for the relevant Year of the Partnership.

(D) Subject to the payment of the sums referred to in sub-clauses (A) and (C) of this Clause, the outgoing partner shall not be entitled to any interest in any of the assets of the Partnership and in particular (but not by way of limitation) he shall not be entitled to any interest in work-in-progress whether or not such work-in-progress appears in the accounts of the Partnership.

(E) The share in the profits of the Partnership of the outgoing partner shall accrue to the continuing Partners in the same relative proportions as those in which they are entitled to the profits of the Partnership at the relevant date and the amount of capital paid out under paragraph (i) of sub-clause (A) of this Clause shall be replaced proportionately by the continuing Partners according to their said respective shares of profits and neither the outgoing partner nor his personal representatives shall be entitled to any further share or interest in the assets or goodwill of the Partnership or in the profits accruing after the relevant date and shall have no claim in respect of the same, the obligations of the other Partners under this Deed being accepted by each of them as full consideration for the acquisition by the continuing Partners of any share or interest in the assets or goodwill or profits of the Partnership to which the outgoing partner might otherwise claim to be entitled.

(F) The outgoing partner shall pay and discharge all debts and liabilities in respect of income tax attributable to the outgoing Partner's share of the profits of the Partnership and a proportion (equal to the proportion in which he was at the relevant date entitled to such profits) of any debt or liability in respect of any claim arising from any wrongful act or omission of the parties hereto or any of them to the extent that such claim is not covered by insurance and shall keep the continuing Partners and their respective estates and effects indemnified against such debts and liabilities and all actions, proceedings, costs, claims and demands in respect thereof.

(G) The outgoing partner or his personal representatives (as the case may be) shall sign, execute and do all such documents, deeds, acts and things as the continuing Partners may reasonably request for the purpose of enabling the continuing Partners to recover and get in the assets of the Partnership.

[* *For an alternative to paragraph (A)(i) see p 153.*]

25 Winding-up of the partnership

Unless on the expiration or determination of the Partnership a majority of the Partners continue in partnership then within [ ] calendar months after the expiration or determination of the Partnership a full and general account in writing shall be taken by the Partners of all the moneys, debts, effects and other assets then belonging or due to the Partnership and of all moneys and debts due by, and of the liabilities of, the Partnership and a just valuation shall be made of all the particulars included in such account which require and are capable of valuation and immediately after such last-mentioned account shall have been so taken and settled the Partners shall forthwith make provision for the payment of all moneys and debts then due by the Partnership and for meeting all the liabilities thereof and subject thereto all the moneys, debts, effects and other assets then belonging or due to the Partnership shall be divided between the Partners according to their respective shares, rights and interest therein and such instruments in writing shall be executed by them respectively for facilitating the getting in of the outstanding debts and effects of the Partnership and for indemnifying each other touching the premises and for vesting the sole right and property in the said respective shares in the said moneys, debts, effects and other assets in the Partners to whom the same respectively shall upon such division belong and for releasing to each other all claims on account of the Partnership accordingly as the circumstances shall require.

26 Expulsion of partners

If any Partner shall:

(i) by act or default commit any flagrant breach of his duties as a Partner or of the agreements and stipulations herein contained; or

(ii) fail to account and pay over or refund to the Partnership any money for which he is accountable to the Partnership within fourteen days after being required so to do by a Partner specifically so authorised by a decision of the Partners; or

(iii) act in any respect contrary to the good faith which ought to be observed between Partners; or

(iv) become subject to the bankruptcy laws; or

(v) enter into any composition or arrangement with or for the benefit of his creditors; or

(vi) be or become permanently incapacitated by mental disorder, ill-health, accident or otherwise from attending to the Partnership business; or

(vii) (except with the consent of the other Partners) absent himself from the said business for more than [ ] calendar months in any one year or for more than [ ] consecutive days (absence during the usual holidays or due to temporary illness or as agreed not being reckoned) then and in any such case the other Partners may by notice in writing given to him or (in the case of his being found incapable, by reason of mental disorder, of managing and administering his property and affairs for the purposes of Section 101 of the Mental Health Act 1959) to his receiver or other appropriate person or left at the office of the Partnership determine the Partnership so far as he may be concerned and publish a notice of dissolution of the Partnership in the name of and as against such Partner whereupon the Partnership will so far as regards such Partner immediately cease and determine accordingly but without prejudice to the remedies of the other Partners for any antecedent breach of any of the stipulations or agreements aforesaid and any question as to a case having arisen to authorise such notice shall be referred to arbitration.

27 Continuance of the partnership for tax purposes

Every outgoing partner or his personal representatives (as the case may be) shall if so requested by the continuing Partners join with them in giving to Her Majesty's Inspector of Taxes a notice under Section 154 of the Taxes Act regarding the continuance of the practice of the Partnership and the outgoing partner and his personal representatives shall be indemnified by the continuing Partners against:

(i) any income tax which may be payable by the outgoing partner or his personal representatives as a result of giving such notice in excess of the income tax which would have been payable if no such notice had been given; and

(ii) any income tax which may be payable by the outgoing partner or his personal representatives as a result of a subsequent change being treated as a permanent discontinuance in excess of the income tax which would have been payable if no subsequent change so treated had taken place.

28 Arbitration

Whenever any doubt, difference or dispute shall arise between the Partners or any of them or between any of them and the personal representatives of any other Partner touching these presents or the construction hereof or any Clause or thing herein contained or any account, valuation or division of assets, debts or liabilities to be made as hereinbefore mentioned or any other thing in any wise relating to or concerning the Partnership Business or the affairs thereof or the rights, duties or liabilities of any party under these presents, the matter in difference shall be referred to a single arbitrator to be agreed upon by the parties or in default of such agreement to be nominated at the request of any such party by the President for the time being of The Law Society and to be a Barrister-at-Law [Solicitor] of not less than ten years' standing. Such arbitration shall be held in London and shall be in accordance with and subject to the provisions of the Arbitration Acts 1950–79.

IN WITNESS whereof this Deed has been entered into the day and year first above written.

SCHEDULE 1

The [Existing] Partners

SCHEDULE 2

The New Partners

SCHEDULE 3

The Salaried Partners

SCHEDULE 4

The Consultants

Index